INDIAN POETRY IN ENGLISH

A Critical Study

Sangita Padhi

ATLANTIC
PUBLISHERS & DISTRIBUTORS (P) LTD

ATLANTIC
PUBLISHERS & DISTRIBUTORS (P) LTD
7/22, Ansari Road, Darya Ganj, New Delhi
Tel.: +91-11-4077 5252, 2327 3880
E-mail: orders@atlanticbooks.com
Web: www.atlanticbooks.com

Reprint 2018, 2026

Published by Atlantic Publishers & Distributors (P) Ltd.

Printed & bound in India by Atlantic Print Services

Preface

The book aims at studying the form and vision in the poetry of Nissim Ezekiel, A.K. Ramanujan, R. Parthasarathy, Jayanta Mahapatra and Kamala Das. It proposes to examine and analyze the various modes and strategies employed by these Indian poets writing in English to construct the concept of home and/or nation in their poetry. The book also discusses the compulsions behind their quest for such construction.

Home assumes a metaphoric and symbolic significance in the poetry of Ezekiel, A.K. Ramanujan, R. Parthasarathy, Jayanta Mahapatra and Kamala Das. All of them share a common home-bound vision as they realize that home and the land of their birth embody human warmth, security, love and affection. In relating themselves to their homes and the nation, these poets find their own identities and reaffirm their faith in human values, family and familial relationship. They come to realize that home is an abode and symbol of security, love, grace and solace. Hence, in their poetry, these poets show an intense earnestness for construction of home and the nation, and all of them share a common vision i.e. the home-bound vision.

The book also examines the form of their poetry by a close reading of the poems, and tries to establish that each of the five poets under study shows his/her deep commitment to the values and traditions of the land he/she is born into, its culture, history and milieu. Most importantly, all of them have skilfully integrated the linguistic and rhetorical resources of both the English language and their mother tongue. Although they use English as their creative medium, they remain bound to their home, society, culture and nation, which authenticate their identity and shape their sensibility.

Indian poetry in English in the post-Independence period has formed a distinctive indigenous tradition of its own. But it would not be possible to examine all the poets who have formed and/or perpetuated such a tradition. For the sake of convenience, the study brings to focus only representative poets of the pre-Independence period and post-Independence period. The poetry of Derozio, Toru Dutt, Aurobindo Ghosh, Sarojini Naidu, and Manmohan Ghose has been examined to throw light on the form and vision of Indian English poetry. The poetry of Nissim Ezekiel, A.K. Ramanujan, R. Parthasarathy, Jayanta Mahapatra, and Kamala Das has been critically analyzed, focusing on their effort to construct the concepts of home and/or nation in their poetry. The book relies on the paradigms of the postcolonial theory to examine the scope and dimension of Indian poetry in English today.

The subject matter is divided into seven chapters. The first chapter focuses on the crux of the thesis, with a historical perspective of the Indian poetry in English from Derozio till date. The chapter also highlights how the English romanticism of the early Indian English poets makes a significant departure in the writings of the poets in the post-Independence and post-colonial period. It briefly discusses the post-colonial strategies and paradigms employed by the poets under study in this book. The second chapter through the sixth analyze and examine the poetry of Ezekiel, A.K. Ramanujan, R. Parthasarathy, Kamala Das and Jayanta Mahapatra individually. In the concluding chapter, an attempt has been made to summarize the findings and observations of the preceding five chapters, in conformity with the vision they share together. A brief study of a couple of other Indian English poets who also share a similar vision of constructing home, community and nation, is appended in the concluding chapter. There is a selected Bibliography at the end. The methodology applied in the book comprises a close reading of the texts and incorporation of the secondary source materials from a post-modern and post-colonial perspective.

The book will be useful for the students and teachers of Indian English literature, especially Indian English poetry and researchers in these fields.

Sangita Padhi

Contents

1

Introduction

The book proposes to study and critically examine the poetry of Nissim Ezekiel, Attipat Krishnaswamy Ramanujan, Rajagopal Parthasarathy, Kamala Das and Jayanta Mahapatra—the major voices in the Contemporary Indian Poetry in English. It attempts to analyse the different modes and strategies employed by these poets to substantiate the view that their poetry makes a persistent effort to construct the concept of home and/or nation and the compulsions behind such construction. Each of these poets pursues the quest for the metaphoric and symbolic dimensions of home/nation, which is central to his/her poetry.

Home/nation, the place of nativity, serve as a backdrop, a bower that encompasses love, grace, human warmth, security and solace—the values that redeem them from agony, despair and anguish. It binds them to the roots and bridges the inner self with the world without. When these poets remain physically away from home, they suffer the pangs of alienation and the loss of identity. In the process of their quest—journey, they came to understand that home is a shield that can protect and preserve their identity. They realize that home is a pilgrimage, a holy place that not only shapes and moulds their personalities, attitudes and visions, but also reveals the value and meaning of their existence. It is only at the institution of home and the place of their nativity, the nation, that these poets come to terms with their "self". Thus, the poetry of Ezekiel, Ramanujan, Parthasarathy, Kamala Das and Jayanta Mahapatra embodies a quest for home/nation with a deep sense of belonging and commitment.

In the socio-cultural context, home stands for love, security and tenderness, kinship and familial relationship, which these poets passionately long for. Their works embody the quest for home and the vision to construct it in the idioms and the forms these poets make use of and the linguistic and aesthetic traditions they belong to. A home may be a social unit or a nation, a geographical region, but it has its own socio-cultural moorings and ethos, tradition and history, religion and myths. It is abode—may it be Ezekiel's Bombay (now Mumbai), Jayanta Mahapatra's Orissa (now Odisha), or the South India of Ramanujan, Parthasarathy and Kamala Das—which shapes the sensibility of the poet and provides him/her a definitive and distinctive identity. The five representative poets of the post-independence era chosen for study in this book willingly pursue their quest for construction of home/nation by understanding their individual self, discard its shortcomings absurdities and infatuations, remain committed to and involved in their roots, their home and native land, their people and history, their culture and their ethos.

II

A brief survey of the critical and scholarly works on Ezekiel, Ramanujan, Parthasarathy, Kamala Das and Jayanta Mahapatra reveals that post-independence Indian English Poetry has attracted substantial critical attention, both in Indian Poetry in English and considerable attempts have also been made to study individual poets. But a comparative and comprehensive study of the above-mentioned poets in relation to their home-bound vision has rarely been attempted.

Lind Hess in her study of *India Poetry in English* in the post-independence era call Ezekiel a "city" poet. She examines the poet's acknowledgment of a "home" in the city of Bombay. K.D. Verma claims that Nissim Ezekiel's poetry is a romantic nostalgia for the lost home, the home of the spirit. Rajeev Taranath and Meena Belliappa emphasize on Ezekiel's urban theme and his search for identity. V.A. Shahane examines the existential dilemma in Ezekiel's poetry and goes on to say that Ezekiel's Jewish mind is influenced by the Hindu thought and philosophy. Bruce King in his book *Modern Indian Poetry in English* analyses Ezekiel's quest for home and his self.

Ramanujan too is variously interpreted and analyzed by a wide range of critics and scholars. K.R. Srinivas Iyengar, a pioneering scholar of Indian writing in English, treats Ramanujan's *Relations* as a bridge between childhood and age, between India and America. Devendra Kohli lays stress on the use of memory in Ramanujan's poems which is aimed at creating Indian ethos. Homi Bhabha examines Ramanujan's falling back on family and familial relationship as a means to align himself with history and tradition. Keki N. Daruwalla observes that Ramanujan's poetry flourishes under the aegis of family tree, with an orthodox Hindu mind. M.K. Naik discusses Ramanujan's intense desire to search for his roots which makes him fall back on memory in a seminal essay, "A.K. Ramanujan and the Search for Roots". Y.N. Vaish sees Ramanujan as an escapist and holds that he escapes from the American environment of the machine culture.

Most critics and scholars have emphasized on the exilic mode of Parthasarathy's poetry, which makes an effort to re-establish the poet's rapport with his own roots. Most critics see in *Rough Passage* a journey and a quest for the poet's Tamil roots. Brijraj Singh evaluates Parthasarathy's bi-cultural and multilingual situation. The poet strives for a living tradition of his native soil to gather strength and vitality. Subhas Shah considers *Rough Passage* as a poem of self-discovery and self-analysis, wherein the poet recreates and recognizes his own self. Bijay Kumar Das highlights the autobiographical element of *Rough Passage*. But Das fails to find out the poet's love and need for a home. Rosaly Puthuceary examines the ambivalence and irony in *Rough Passage* and holds that it is ironical for Parthasarathy to use English as the medium to overcome or resolve the dilemma. M.K. Naik, however, in his seminal book *A History of Indian English Literature* finds out the journey—motif in *Rough Passage*, which he calls "a journey within".

In his essay, "R. Parthasarathy: Images of a Poet" Roger Iredale finds out three stages of the Poet's emotional and intellectual development in the three sections of *Rough Passage*, which finds fulfilment in the final return to home.

Similarly, Jayanta Mahapatra and Kamala Das have drawn serious critical attention both at home and aboard. But their home-bound vision or their zeal to construct the concept of home/nation has been grossly overlooked. Professor K.R.S. Iyengar in Indian writing in English opines that Mahapatra's poems, particularly relationship, are real achievements. There is neither "waiting" not any "false start", but triumphant "arriving". V.A. Shahane in the poetry of Jayanta Mahapatra, holds that Mahapatra attempts to build a fugue-like structure that evokes the myths and traditions of Orissa. The poet articulates the sensitive responses of his self to the tradition of Orissa, its myths, legends and its rich architectural and sculptural treasures. M.K. Naik reviewing Jayanta Mahapatra's poetry in *Indian Book Chronicle*, January, 1983, says that the myth, legend and history of his land find stronger presence in his poems. D.S. Rao and Ajit Khullar maintain that Mahapatra borrows heavily from several sources. Even voices like those of Whitman, Coleridge, Keats, Yeats and Eliot buzz in his poems. Kamala Das has received wide publicity and have reviews for her lobe poems where her feminine sensibility, according to Bijay Kumar Das, finds its finest and fullest expression. Critics and scholars over that her nationality and identity are to be found in being rooted in the Indian soil. Devendra Kohli maintains that Kamala Das's response to the landscape of her country, her sense of tradition and culture of the land of her birth go together to make an identity of her own. Both William Walsh and Bijay Kumar Das find her attitude defiant. Courage, conviction and honesty are the hallmark of her poetry. Eunice de Souza projects her inner sense of dirt and sexual disgust, the anger, anguish and agony of her married life that compels her to long for the lost innocence and childhood at her Nalapat house in Malabar. What de Souza appreciates and admires is Kamala Das's free, frank and fearless expression of love and feminine sensibility.

The present book has taken note of all the scholarly and critical voices with particular reference to the five poets chosen for study. Although the theme of çommitment to the place or roots and the quest for identity is independently or variously examined and analysed, no attempt has hitherto been made to project the kind of common vision all of them share, i.e. to construct the concept of home/nation. Hence, this study makes an attempt to club together Ezekiel, Ramanujan, Parthasarathy, Jayanta Mahapatra and Kamala Das in terms of their vision vis-à-vis their poetic forms and craft. The present work further tries to establish that Indian Poetry in English has taken firm roots in the Indian subcontinent, in its home, and that it has carved in an indigenous tradition.

III

Indian poetry in English has established itself globally as a distinctive genre with the pioneering works by Nissim Ezekiel, A.K. Ramanujan, R. Parthasarathy, Kamala Das and Jayanta Mahapatra in the post-independence period. However, the use of English language as a means to express native ethos can be traced back to the first quarter of the 19th century, when Henry Derozio published a volume of poems in English in 1827, wherein the poet registered his patriotic fervor and his sense of belonging to India. Since then, English has no longer been the language of the Britons alone, rather it has become the language of the intellectuals and the creative medium of writers all over the world in the 20th century and after.

Indian poets and writers of the post-independence era have developed an indigenous tradition in English language by motivating and approaching it to suit to their purpose. They use English as their creative medium by constructing an Indian context and Indianness so that English language has acquired a distinctive identity in the hands of the Indian poets and writers. These men of letters have absorbed and assimilated English language with their native soil and in the process, they have nativised and acclimatized the language. Although they use English as the medium, "there is a sensibility that is identified with the land and the people of India" (Paniker 137).

Indian English poetry owes its origin to Henry Derozio's "Poems" published in 1827, Derozio (1809-31) was born and brought up in Calcutta (now Kolkata). His poetry voices Indian national zeal and a sense of belonging to his place, Derozio makes use of Indian theme, myths and legends, imagery and diction. In "My Native Land" Derozio sings of India and its glorious past:

> My country! in the day of glory past
>
> A beauteous halo circled rained the brow,
>
> And worshipped as a deity thou wast,
>
> Where is that glory, where that reverence now?
>
> (Prasad 1994: 47)

It is through his poetry that Derozio sings the glory of his motherland India. He was the first Indian English poet to give vent to his patriotism and sing of freedom. He was modern India's first poet to contemplate on intellectual renaissance for his nation.

Between Derozio and Ezekiel, there are few Indian English poets, such as Kashi Prasad Ghosh, Michael Madhusudan Dutt, Toru Dutt, Manmohan Ghose, Nab Kishen Ghose, Sri Aurobindo, Harindranath Chattopadhyay and Sarojini Naidu, who accepted English language as a medium to communicate. Kashi Prasad Ghosh (1803-73) Published a volume of English poems which mainly dealt with various Hindu festivals and social practices. Michael Madhusudan Dutt (1824-73), whom Parthasarathy calls "the paradigm of the Indian poet writing in English and he tries to explain the west in Indian terms" (Parthasarathy 4), has left behind him *Visions of the Past* (1848) and *Captive Ladie* (1849) as his legacy of poetic work. Dutt imitated the blank verse of Lord Byron and experimented with the English sonnet form.

Nab Kishen Ghose (1837-1918), who catalogued his own religious attitude and mythical experiences through poetic forms, tried to explore his self in his poetry. Toru Dutt (1856-77) was one of the versatile poets of colonial India. Born and brought up in Kolkata, she travelled in Europe (France, Italy and England) in her for native years of 15 to 19. Her initial attempt was translating French poems into English. Then she composed her own lyrics and retold in English the stories and songs from her own mother tongue. The English Romantic poets were her models, and she draw heavily on the early 19th century poetry for her imagery and symbols. In Ancient Ballads and Legends of Hindustan, published posthumously in 1882, Toru Dutt employs native Indian colour, and the poem speaks of Dutt's love of nature, sorrow over the destruction of nature and her nostalgia. Paul verges has rightly observed: "Toru Dutt made an effort to reveal the soul of India through the medium of poetry by narrating stories sung in divine poetry thousands of years ago" (29). Besides writing poetry, Toru Dutt also wrote in English the stories of Druba and Prahalada, Sita and Savitri—the mythological figures adored in every Indian household.

For Aurobindo Ghose (1872-1950), Poetry is the 'Mantra of the Real'. A spiritual seeker, Aurobindo's concept of poetry springs from his Yogic experiences. 'Savitri', his epic poem, is composed in 2400 lines in English, which carries a deep spiritual reality. Its mystical content bears the stamp of Indian consciousness and sensibility. His love for his country is best defined when he holds that the Indian nation is not a piece of earth, nor a figure of speech, or a fiction of the mind; it is a mighty Shakti. Aurobindo was a distinguished Indian poet in English and an outstanding critic, whom C.D. Narasimhaiah often compared with Joseph Conrad: "Like Conrad...Sri Aurobindo made the English language accommodate certain hitherto unknown areas of experience..." (Narasimhaiah 29).

Sarojini Naidu (1879-1949), the Nightingale of India, is a poet par excellence. Her poetry is lyrical and melodious, she uses a basket full of similes and metaphors in her poetry. She draws her images from the native sources of myths, legends and fold loves that make her poetry enchantingly delicious. Srinivasa Iyengar rightly calls her the "Indian Elizabeth Barret Browning". Sarojini's famous line, "the bridal songs and cradle songs have cadences of sorrow" evoke sheer melody, or "Rise, Mother, rise, regenerate from gloom/ And, like a bride high rated with the spheres/ Beget new glories from thine ageless womb!" from the poem "To India" shows the poet's courage and patriotic zeal. She not only reminds Mother India of her past glory, but also pines to restore her lost pride and resurrect her from the colonial hegemony.

Of these poets, only Toru Dutt, Sri Aurobindo and Sarojini Naidu stand out as significant contributors to the realm of Indian English poetry. But, Toru Dutt and Sarojini Naidu imitated the British poets, and Aurobindo was more a mystic and a yogi than a poet. However, these three poets are considered to be our most well known and substantial poets in the pre-independence period. They were true nationalists and patriots, and their poetry bear undercurrents of resistance to the colonial rule. Paul Varghese observes that the poets in the pre-independence era expressed "the personality of India through their verse" (Varghese 93). If Sarojini Naidu, Toru Dutt, Derozio and Aurobindo evolved an idiom of their own, it was because these poets realized that "English...is a language of modern India in which words and expressions have recognized national rather than imported significances and references, alluding to local realities, traditions and ways of feeling" (King 1987: 3).

IV

After India achieved independence and the Commonwealth group of nations was formed in the post-1950 period, the whole poetic scenario changed in the Indian subcontinent. Ezekiel's *A Time to Change* published in 1952 heralded a new era of modernism in Indian English poetry. Indian poetry in English as a distinct genre emerged in the poetry of Nissim Ezekiel, Kamala Das and A.K. Ramanujan in the 1960s. R. Parthasarathy's *Ten Twentieth Century Indian Poets* published in 1976 marked the beginning of Post Modernism in Indian English poetry, Jayanta Mahapatra's *Relationship*, Ezekiel's *Latter-Day Psalms*, Kamala Das's *Collected Poems* and A.K. Ramanujan's *Collected Poems* embody the characteristic of postmodernism and post-colonialism in the last two decades of the 20th century.

These poets have given Indian English poetry a definite direction, a distinctive Indianized idiom and a sense of purpose—they have created an indigenous tradition for poetry. English has been their language of self-discovery. By communicating with and reaching out the larger audience in this medium, they valorize the past glory, cluture, tradition and million of the place they are born into, and this decolonize the mind. The post-independence Indian English poets authenticate their identity in relation to their roots, their home, their nation. Hence, in all their poetry there is a common vision—the home-bound vision and a sense of need to construct the concept of home and/or nation. They try to achieve the goal in their poetry by nativizing the English language and using it as a vehicle to express their feelings, emotions and experiences with an Indian sensibility and flavour.

Nissim Ezekiel's Jewish background makes him a natural outsider but he has chosen Bombay/India his home and for him: Home is where you gather grace ('Enterprise' 118). Although born in a Ben Israel Jew family in Bombay, Ezekiel considers himself an Indian, and India, "a loved and troubled country" is simply his environment and his home. He remains home-bound through his total involvement with Bombay, the miniature secular India. His poetry manifests the lives, identities, culture and tradition, the past and the present of the people inhabiting his adopted home.

On the physical level, home for Ezekiel is the centre of one's identity. It is the repository of love, affection, human warmth and relationship. Ezekiel's poetry celebrates his commitment to Bombay—the literal or physical home of the poet. It is through an open-hearted commitment his place as well as his active understanding of and involvement with the people, their culture, their ethos that Ezekiel redefines his identity as an Indian. On the aesthetic level, home is the symbol of an integrated personality so that his vision of constructing home/nation keeps intensified. It is through home-bound vision that Ezekiel comes to terms with his self. Ezekiel looks into his own self through poetry. In an interview he says:

> Within the general urge to change which
> Ought to mean to improve, and not merely
> To become different, my poetry has certain

Helped me. It has been like a good adviser,
A competent therapist. My poetry has helped
Me discover my faults and weakness,
Though not always to conquer them (Hoskote 8)

And, on the spiritual level, home becomes the symbol of purification. Ezekiel's spiritual quest originates from and is moulded by his Jewish consciousness and the Bible. His Jewish background and religion enable him to establish a rapport with his ancestors, his roots and his origin. It has helped him achieve equanimity and quietude, and thus resolve his problem of identity. Hence, a persistent striving to lean home/nation ward or construct the home/community/nation in Ezekiel's poetry.

A.K. Ramanujan and R. Parthasarathy try to construct their concept of home and/or nation by relating to their roots, their family and familial relationships and the traditions of their place of origin i.e. the South India. Although Ramanujan has settled in the U.S.A. with an America citizenship, the chief motif of his quest if embedded in India, his home and his nation. On the other hand, Parthasarathy, in the early part of his career, becomes infatuated with England and English language but he rightly realizes the futility of such infatuation. He recognizes the meaningfulness and significance of his roots, his home and the land of his birth, which have shaped and moulded his sensibility and his vision. He comes back to India, to his home and his family and reaffirms his faith in it.

Both Ramanujan and Parthasarathy try to revitalize their in effable rapport with India. At the familial or physical level. Ramanujan shows his total commitment to the Tamil past, and at the linguistic level he falls back on the classical Tamil and Kannada literary traditions. Parthasarathy to remains committed to his Tamils roots both in the personal as well as linguistic level to resolve his problem of identity and alienation. Both Parthasarathy and Ramanujan, in order to redefine their identity, try to mould the English language to form an indigenous tradition in Indian English poetry. In fact, Ramanujan becomes the first Indian poet in English to create a native tradition in Indian English. Both Ramanujan and Parthasarathy felt that

English language must be enriched by the resources of the native languages in order to give it a distinct in Indian identity.

Ramanujan, in particular, follows the stylistic elements of classical Tamil Poetry, and he makes use of all the signalling and significant constituents of form and style available in Tamil classics. His use of irony and the insets of imagery give him scope to integrate form and meaning and vision of his poetry.

In an interview with a group of Tamil writers, Ramanujan states: "I prefer the classical. A typical 'Sangam' poem has a well-defined well-wrought complex form" ("A Meeting" 11), in another interview with Ramnath Jha, Ramanujan candidly admits: "my poem Morgan, for instance, could not have been written if I didn't know classical Tamil forms and even some of the images there" (Jha 7).

Thus, both incorporated into their English certain strategies and devices drawn from classical Tamil and Kannada poetry, thereby giving Indian English its legitimacy and roots.

Living in an alien soil of America, Ramanujan confronts the problem of alienation and identity crisis. By falling back on his personal and familial past, Ramanujan perpetuates his quest for his roots, his home and family and tries to overcome his identity crisis. Although he stays in America, his heart lives in India. Like Ramanujan, Parthasarathy too relapses into the repository of his familial past and remains committed to his native tradition and lives to resolve the problem of identity and alienation. His initial disenchantment with India dies down and he reaffirms his faith in his home and homeland. The values associated with his home and land of his birth appear meaningful. His disenchantment with the British Raj and his feeling of being an exile in a free India initially gives him a false promise of home. But his gradual initiation of a dialogue with his Tamil past and his final acceptance of home as the source of love, solace and security constitute Parthasarathy's vision of construction his home or his home-bound vision. After a brief and temporary meandering on the English corridors, he finally comes back to his native soil where his roots are embedded. In his essay "Whoring After English Gods", Parthasarathy admits that he was "hypocritical of everything Indian" and that "England would be his future home and English language would help him belong there" (Parthasarathy 43-44). But his hopes soon withered and died down.

In *Rough Passage* he says:

> My tongue in English chains
>
> I return, after a generation to you. (49)

This marks Parthasarathy's total commitment to and his identification with his home, his country and the Tamil literary tradition into which he was born.

Kamala Das (1934-2009) is the best known Indian woman poet writing in English. She is firmly rooted in the Indian soil, and she claims that she and her poetry both are Indian, not Western. She writes:

> I am Indian, very brown, born in Malabar,
>
> I speak in three languages, write in Two, dream in one....
>
> (*The Old Play House and Other Poems* 59)

Kamala Das has felt the pulse of the whole India, and she draws her imaginative source from her own life's experiences and observations. Unhappy in married life and frustrated in love, she seeks for an escape from the despair and chaotic situations experienced by her female self. Kamala Das's frank expression of her feminine sensibility is the halmark of her love poems.

Das writes poems of her roots, background, about her Nalapat house—her home in Malabar, its inmates and near and dear ones. She perpetuates her home-bound vision as she glorifies the values held dear by home, domesticity and family life. The intimacy of relationship that binds the family finds expression in her poems written on the Nalapat house, on Malabar, on her grandmother and her childhood experience. Kamala Das's fond recollection of the grandmother's love in her poem "My Grandmother's House" is search for relationship. Her escape to her childhood experience shows her longing for innocence and similarity which she has long lost in her Nalapat house. Her depiction of her close intimacy with the grandmother, her sharing of blissful moments and togetherness with her relates to her intimacy with the Nalapat house, her home in her native land Malabar. The vision of her home and the desire to construct it gets enlivened in her and excites her—making her nostalgic and reminiscent in "A hot noon in Malabar". Even when she is ill and lies on the hospital bed with myocarditis and a heart attack, she longs to go back to her Malabar home.

Kamala Das is conscious of her inner void, which she relates to the vacancy of Nalapat house. It hurts her to the core for which she pines to build it, to construct it. Her poetry registers her love for Malabar and India. Indian sensibility forms the core of her poetry. Indian landscape, myths and legends play a dominant role in her poetry. The use of Radha Krishan myth is appealing, as she writes:

> Everything in me
> Is melting, even the hardness at the core
> O Krishna, I am melting, melting
> Nothing remains but you.... (*The Descendants* 9)

Kamala Das's involvement with and use of this traditional myth from the Hindu religious scripture helps her create an identity of her own. She is perhaps the best and perfect among the post-independence Indian English poets to Indianise the English language by incorporating easy colloquial idioms and writing poetry in a lucid, conversational tone, as an Indian reads, writes or perhaps understands. In *The Old Playhouse and Other Poems*, she writes:

> Language I speak
> Becomes mine, its distortions, its queerness,
> All mine, mine alone, it is half-English,
> Half Indian, funny perhaps, but it's honest,
> It is human as I am human,
> Didn't you see? (59)

Thus, Kamala Das's choice of English as her creative medium reinforces her identity, her distinctiveness and rootedness as an Indian. There is in her an earnestness to remain home-bound, roof-bound and a zeal to construct home, family and the nation she is part of Jayanta Mahapatra (1928-) is the first Indian poet in English to be honoured with the Central Sahitya Academy Award for his book *Relationship* in 1981. While speaking at the award giving ceremony Mahapatra spoke of his deep allegiance to his roots, Orissa the place of his birth:

> To Orissa, to the land in which my roots lie and lies my past, and in which lies my beginning and my end, where the wind keens over the great grief of the river Daya and where the waves of the Bay of Bengal fail to reach out today to the twilight soul of Konark, I acknowledge my relationship. (Mohanty 11)

Mahapatra began his poetic career in 1966 writing love poems, but soon came to realize that the theme of live is not enough and that a creative writer cannot exist in a world of dreams and abstractions alone. He began to feel the pull of his roots and tried to establish his rapport with the land of his birth, its people and its landscapes, its ancestral culture and tradition of which he is a vital part. In a dehumanizing post-modern world, Mahapatra hopes that relationships and human bondages can be sustained by trying to be rooted and bound to the place where one is born and brought up.

Childhood memories and reminiscences of the past constantly haunt Mahapatra. His poetry deals with the fleeting nature of time, mortality of self and the fear of death. When the tyranny of the present hangs heavy, Mahapatra feels that it is the historical sense of time and redeeming nature of the past that heals us of our private wounds. The poet goes down the corridors of his ancestral past to trace his identity, search his roots and his origin. Therein lies Mahapatra's earnest quest for home. In his poem "Grandfather", the poet pays tribute to his grandfather. In "From Orissa Landscapes", he recollects a touching moment of his childhood days:

> A long time ago
> A cut my chin and bled,
> My mother clumsily held a lump of sugar
> Against the wound
> To stop the ooze of lice. (122)

In "Way of the River", Mahapatra, while moving on the banks of the river, finds traces of his identity in the flow of the river and realizes that exists because of the graceful benediction of his father and forefathers. Mahapatra's ancestral past—racial or familial—has greatly shaped his vision. He recapitulates and revitalizes the lost dimensions in order to relate himself and identify himself with Orissa, his home.

Mahapatra remains perpetually home-bound by his total identification and involvement with Orissan culture and its myth and tradition. Lord Jagannath at Puri is the centre of Orissa's religio-cultural heritage; the Sun Temple at Konark stands as an emblem of Orissan artistic and architectonic perfection; and the River Daya still glorifies on its banks the valour of Orissan people who died fighting the great Kalinga war against the invincible Emperor Ashoka. Thus, by imaging forth his native land, its milieu and landscapes, its history and culture, its religion and tradition, Mahapatra intensifies his relational integrity to his home in particular and to Orissa in general.

V

The book banks on the paradigms of the post-colonial theory in order to examine the scope and dimension of the poetry of Nissim Ezekiel, Ramanujan, R. Parthasarathy, Kamala Das and Jayanta Mahapatra. These poets have carved a separate space for themselves in the post-independence and post-colonial era, they have developed a new style and a new way of writing in English by indigenizing the form and content. They glorify the culture, tradition, religion and ethos of the land of their birth. In fact, they rediscover their home, their country through their writing.

English education and European culture influenced and enlightened them, but these poets in particular, and the post-independence writers in general, try to define and redefine themselves as native writers through their creative writing. They have challenged the colonizer's language by nativizing the English and adopted it to suit to their literary creation. They express their own sense of identity by shaping and moulding English language to accommodate their ideas and observations.

All of them—Ezekiel, Ramanujan, Parthasarathy, Jayanta Mahapatra and Kamala Das—echo an Indian consciousness that is embedded in the Indian tradition.

The poets chosen for study in the present thesis have heralded a new linguistic tradition which is a typical post-colonial approach. They make rampant use of local words and idioms, indigenous metaphors, and often the form and style of classical Indian literature. Much before the rule of the British empire came to an end, Raja Rao in his foreword to the novel Kanthapura wrote:

> We cannot write like the English. We should not, we cannot write only as Indians. We have grown to look at the large world as part of us. One method of expression therefore has to be a dialect which will someday prove to be as distinctive and colourful as the Irish or American. (5)

Raja Rao, Mulk Raj Anand and R.K. Narayan were the three pioneering Indian English writers who heralded and indigenous tradition in Indian English and offered a literary and linguistic resistance to the empire as early as 1930s. They intended to show the world that the literature of India is different from their British masters.

This process of offering resistance to the colonial ethos and emancipating the suppressed Indian ego, the spirit of breaking away from the British and redefining traditional Indian culture are variously documented in postcolonial paradigms, such as "writing back", "rewriting" and "re-reading", which surfaced in the writing of Kamala Markandaya, Manohar Malgaonkar, Anita Desai and Nayantara Sahgal in the 1960s, and perpetuated in the poetry of Nissim Ezekiel, Ramanujan, Parthasarathy, Kamala Das and Jayanta Mahapatra. During 1980s and 90s and after, writers like Salman Rushdie, Vikram Seth, Arun Joshi, G.V. Desani, Amitav Ghosh, Upamanya Chatterji, Arundhati Roy, Jhumpa Lahiri, Kiran Desai and others have produced prominent postcolonial literature and have proved that India is a significant literary nation in the world.

VI

The book seeks to suggest that Indian poetry in English in the post-independence era has been firmly rooted in the Indian subcontinent and it has established a distinctive indigenous tradition of its own. The study further posits that if Indian poetry in English is to continue to achieve distinction, it has to imbibe a home/nation-bound vision both in theme and in form. The five major representative poets under study here—Ezekiel, A.K. Ramanujan, R. Parthasarathy, Kamala Das and Jayanta Mahapatra bear a common vision and reveal a similar concern for home/nation and reveal a similar concern to reconstruct it at the symbolic and metaphoric level. Their adherence to the roots, to the home, family and the land of their birth constitute the shaping spirit of their poetry. Each one of these poets delves deep into his/her cultural milieu with an attempt to redefine his/her identity. The chapters that follow make an effort to study the poets individually focusing on their theme, style and technique in the perspective of their home/nation-bound vision. The concluding chapter shall attempt to sum up the findings of the preceding chapters, which will be followed by a select bibliography-cum-works cited.

2

Nissim Ezekiel

Nissim Ezekiel (1924-2004) the patriarch of Indian English poetry, is indisputable the foremost among the post-independence Indian poets writing in English. The pioneer, the "Law-giver" (Karnani 9), "the first Indian poet consistently to show Indian readers that craftsmanship is as important to a poem as its subject matters" (Jusawalla 69), "the first Indian poet to have a professional attitude". Nissim Ezekiel "brought a sense of discipline, self-criticism and mastery" (King 91), to Indian poetry in English. Apart from being a very sensitive poet, Ezekiel is also a highly perceptive critic and a source of inspiration for the younger poets of contemporary India. Others wrote verse as a hobby, something that is done in spare moments, but, Ezekiel made it central to his life. He brought a sense of discipline, self-criticism and mastery to Indian English poetry. Ezekiel remains not merely a great creative writer in his own right, but a promoter, a law-giver and above all, the father of modern Indian poetry in English. Like other post-colonial writers, Ezekiel tries to valorize his language, culture, tradition, ethos and sensibility of the land he inhabits.

This chapter attempts to study the multiple facets of Ezekiel's poetry with a view to substantiating the view that he is essentially a home-bound pilgrim like other post-colonial poets of the once colonized country. The post-colonial poets give importance to their home, with all its ramifications and implications. Ezekiel, as a post-colonial poet, also shows these qualities, both in terms of the metaphoric journey and the verbalized quest in his writing. In his poems home/nation occupies a central position in the creative process.

Indian English poetry emerged as a distinct genre in the writings of Nissim Ezekiel, Kamala Das and A.K. Ramanujan in the 1960s. Ezekiel's *A Time to Change* heralded moderation in Indian English poetry. In fact, Ezekiel is to Indian English poetry what T.S. Eliot is to English poetry. He has given Indian English poetry a new direction, an idiom and a sense of purpose besides popularizing it in India and aboard.

Ezekiel is keenly aware of his Jewish background. Though an 'outsider', Ezekiel has attempted to "associate himself with the modern India" (Reddy 6). Being a Jew and raised as a secular rationalist by his scientist father made him an outsider to Hindu-Muslim culture; it is the very outsiderness, his marginality, that makes him a representative voice of the urbanized, Western educated Indians (King 92). Ezekiel's sense of alienation evolves out of his Ben-Israeli origin. In the midst of the Hindus, perhaps the Jew in Ezekiel fails to establish a total sense of relatedness with India.

Born in Bombay in 1924, he completed his primary education in a missionary school and graduated with a Master's degree in English from Bombay University in 1947. Before leaving for England, he taught English literature at Khalasa College. During his stay in England, he had published his first book of poems *A Time to Change* (1952). After his return; his books *Sixty Poems* (1953) and *The Third* (1959) were published, followed by the next two volumes of poems *The Unfinished Man* (1960) and *The Exact Name* (1965). In 1976, he published *Hymns in Darkness* and *Latter-Day Psalms* (1982). Besides writing poetry and teaching English literature, he engaged himself in writing plays, editing journals, delivering lectures on art and literature throughout the world. He has received worldwide fame as a major voice in postcolonial Indian English poetry.

In an interview, Ezekiel clarifies the role of his Jewish origin vis-à-vis his relationship with India:

> I have never wholly identified myself with 'the Indian sensibility' nor do I feel alienated from it now. I have

> always believed that I have particular relationship with that sensibility, which is part of my normal life. No one would accept any alleged 'identification' with it by me and that charge of alienation I consider at the other extreme of interpretation. I am related to, not identified with, not alienated from. (Reddy 6)

Ezekiel's sense of belonging and commitment to India lies embedded in the present, post-independence India. It is through an intense awareness of the spirit of the time and space that a writer obtains the authenticity of his perceptions and vision. In an interview, Ezekiel advocates for this kind of intimate and intense relationship between the writer and the place he is born into:

> A writer needs a national or cultural identity, without that you become a series of limitations, echoes, responses, but you do not develop because there is nothing at the core to develop. ("Interview" *Indian Literary Review* 3)

Ezekiel relates himself to India, and particularly to the city of Bombay (now Mumbai) which embodies his cultural identity:

> I regard myself essentially as an Indian poet writing in English. I have a strong sense of belonging, not only to India, but to this city. (Boston 89)

Ezekiel has accepted Bombay—the cosmopolitan city—the miniature India as his home where life generally is of a uniform tone, irrespective of differences in religious faiths. If Ramanujan and Parthasarathy perpetuate their quest for roots embedded in the tradition they belong to, Ezekiel's journey is within the self, in quest of a spiritual vision that transforms the natural outsider into an instinctive settler. Ezekiel in his autobiographical poem 'Background, causally' articulates the nature of his relationship with India. It is a profound relationship, evolving out of the crisis of identity and need for a home:

> The Indian landscape sears my eyes
>
> I have become a part of it.
>
> I have made my commitments now.
>
> This is one to stay where I am,

As others choose to give themselves in
In some remote an backward place.
My backward place is where I am.
(*Hymns in Darkness* 13)

Ezekiel shows his commitment to India as a conscious act and sees that one must consciously affirm one's Indianness. He chose, publicly and privately, to belong it. His poetry is primarily rooted in urban experiences and asserts his Indianness and his intense relationship with India, particularly with the city of Bombay. He does not want to leave Bombay, his place of birth and his abode. The temptation to escape away rather than into is ever present and yet ever resisted. Hence he writes in "The Egoist's Prayers":

Confiscate my passport, Lord.
I don't want to go aboard.
Let me find my song
Where I belong. (*Hymns* 49)

This is the fact that—English language may take you aboard, may give you an opportunity to settle elsewhere but the passport is Indian, reminding you of where you belong. It shows Ezekiel as a leading nationalist, who owes more to his home, his motherland.

The city occupies a central position in the creative mind of Ezekiel. His attitude to India/Bombay is complex. In fifth of the Poster poems he writes:

I've never been a refuge
Except of the spirit,
A loved and troubled country
Which is my home and enemy.

Paradoxically, the city that is filled with the hope of love is "sick with slums" and beggars:

Barbaric city sick with slums,
Deprived of seasons, blessed with rains,
Its hawkers, beggars, iron-lunged,
Processions led by frantic drums,

A million purgatorial lanes,
And child-like masses, many-tongued,
Whole wages are in words and crumbs.
(*The Unfinished Man*)

The allegorical images of Bombay are perhaps reflected in this poem.

Linda Hess in her perceptive study of Indian poetry in English makes an insightful observation on Ezekiel's urban theme and the theme of commitment. She writes:

> He is a poet of the city, Bombay; a poet of the body; and an endless explorer of the labyrinths of the mid, the devious delving and twisting of the ego, and the ceaseless attempt of man and poet to define himself and to find through 'the myth and maze' a way to honesty and love. (Hess 30)

Thus for Ezekiel, the city is not only a physical presence that impinges on his consciousness, but also a formal trope that leads him to the exploration of the existential self.

Kamala Das constantly employs the metaphor of the city for life, as in the poem "A New City". There is an anguished awareness on her part to have lost something in adopting the city as her home. She discovers that 'all the Delhi streets' are 'fragrant and murky' rendering her 'very young, very lovely and delightfully carefree'. She contrasts the peace of the Delhi landscape with the disturbed mind. When she bids farewell to the city of her long residence, Bombay, which she loves so deeply:

I take leave of you, fair city, while tears
Hide somewhere in my adult eyes
And sadness is silent as a stone

Ezekiel on the other hand not shown such type of painful parting of a loved one, though the city of Bombay forms an integral part of the emotional make-up of the poet. He becomes a part of this subcontinent where he fuses his past, present and future. He accepts Bombay as his home and declares:

I cannot leave the island,
I was born here and belong.

Even now a host of miracles
Hurries me to daily business,
Minding the ways of the island,
As a good native should,
Taking calm and clamour in my stride. (*Hymns* 14)

Thus Bombay, the seed-bed of Ezekiel's corporeal being constitutes the guiding metaphor of his search for home, his roots.

The city of Bombay places high in his diary and make the poet affirm his faith in it. As a result, the city is elevated to the symbolic height of a protector.

Ezekiel's 'Something to Pursue' celebrates this symbolic significance of the city as a protector, a redeemer. After touching the breasts of harlots, the poet comes back to the city to beg forgiveness. For the poet's contrite heart it is only the city that can bring some solace.

City becomes a saviour for him:

To save myself
From what the city had made of me I returned
As intended, to the city I had known.
(*A Time to Change* 18)

In a sequence of thirty poems, "Edinburgh Interludes, Lightly", Ezekiel acknowledges his deep allegiance to the city. These poems, written during his visit to London and Edinburgh in the summer of 1893, celebrate and authenticate the Indian experience with such passion that Ezekiel eminently deserves to be christened as a home-bound pilgrim. Wherever he goes, he bears within him the seeds of home. Bombay has taken such an enormous shape in Ezekiel's consciousness that its evasion is impossible:

I have not come
to Edinburgh
to remember
Bombay mangoes,
But I remember them,

even as I look
at the monument
To sir Walter Scott,
Or stroll along
in the hermitage of Braid.
Perhaps it is not the mangoes
that my eyes and tongue long for
but Bombay as the fruit
On which I've lived
winning and losing
my little life. (*Collected Poems* 293)

Such a gesture can be termed as postcolonial, which negates centre but accepts the life as it is. Ezekiel authenticates his life, shaped by his place of birth as 'fruit', that he lived 'winning' and 'losing'. He not only tries to valorize the place of birth, but also the life it provides to him.

Gieve Patel appropriately writes in the introduction to Ezekiel's *Collected Poems*:

> The poets continued identification with this country is seen to have been the correct choice for him, sustaining him as writer and human being; ending with an acknowledgement that his own personal backwardness as a man, and the ostensible backwardness of the country, are one and the same thing. (xxiii)

In the very first poem of the sequence Ezekiel admits that his allegiance to the city is a fact or existence:

I have become
Part of the scene
Which I can neither love nor hate.
(*Collected Poems* 289)

He is equally aware of the unsavoury elements of the busy metropolis. The enormity of the city's problems makes the poet feel helpless. Although Ezekiel's preoccupation with the city as a dominating metaphor embodies the true nature of his commitment, he does not remain blind to its multiple problems. The city is without love; its men and women are routine-bound, selfish. Ezekiel in his poem, "Boss" images forth the hypnotic impact of the city on the people through the person of an executive:

> Above the bent and busy head the fan turns;
> the dream-window stares back into the busy room.
> No fire burns but bells ring-Hours move on small routines
> Around the bent and busy head.
> The dream-window stares again
> At small routines, the fat turns, No fire burns but bells ring-
> Till time is worn out to the bone. (*Sixty Poems* 9)

The city is an abode of many hungers. People visit hotels and bars with an ulterior motive of enjoying sexuality. In "At the Hotel" Ezekiel reflects on the banal attitude of the city-dwellers:

> Our motives were concealed but clear,
> Not coffee but the Cuban dancer took us there,
> The naked Cuban dancer
> One the dot she came and shook her breasts
> All over us and dropped
> The thin transparent skirt she wore.
> (*Collected Poems* 112)

Ezekiel harps on the complete breakdown of values in his city. The carve for flesh and body's glitter and sputter eats away the city-dweller's moral strength. In a good number of poems of the "Unfinished Man", Ezekiel registers the city-dweller's uncanny and pitiless existence. A city-dweller is divorced from the bliss and quietude of the natural surroundings. The city makes people heartless, selfish. People do not have sympathy for the poor, the downtrodden and even for the animals. In 'Entertainment' Ezekiel depicts the selfish attitude of the city-dwellers who live "away from beach and tree and stone" (*Collected Poems* 117). Monkey-show is a common sight in the cities. 'The girl', 'the baby', 'the two monkeys clad in red and purple pantaloons' and the 'master of ceremonies', 'naked to the waist'—all display their tricks to entertain the city-dwellers. With the sound of the drum people encircle the monkey show. They, however, leave the spot when the time for payment comes. The poet aptly sums up the show and irony of the situation:

> Only the monkeys are sad,
> And suddenly
> The baby begins to cry.
> Anticipating time for payment,
> The crowd dissolves
> Some, in shame, part
> With the smallest coin they have.
> The show moves on. (*Hymns* 27)

The city as a metaphor, living and vital, grows in concomitance with the poet's mature vision:

> Always in the sun's eye,
> Here among the beggars
> Hawkers, pavement sleepers,
> Hutment dwellers, slums,
> Dead souls of men and Gods,
> Burnt-out mothers, frightened
> Virgins, wasted child
> And tortured animal,
> All in noisy silence
> Suffering the place and time. (*Collected Poems* 131)

The city, a miniature India, a miniature world for Ezekiel, becomes s symbol of corruption, dehumanization.

Painfully he admits:

> I am corrupted by the world, continually
> Reduced to something less than something human
> By the crowd, Newspapers, cinemas, radio-features,
> (*A Time to Change* 8)

Adil Jussawalla rightly comments on the ingenuity of Ezekiel's use of city as a metaphor of decay, degeneration, moral vacuity, and living death:

> The city becomes hell and it is one of Ezekiel's achievements that without being quaintly lurid or straining for exotic effects, he represents it as the hopeless Indian hell it is. (Jussawalla 79-80)

Thus the city for Ezekiel remains "a dehumanized and infernal abode" (Varma 232). Yet it is an abode, a home from where "we have to gather grace" (*The Unfinished Man*).

In course of time, as Ezekiel matures as a man and a citizen of the metropolis of Bombay, his aesthetic vision as an artist intensifies. He endears this hell as his abode; he endears darkness for it has its own inner solacing grandeur and delight. He endears the city and its oddities. He learns to accept life as it is and embrace things as they are:

> There's one thing to be said for hell:
>
> It's a pretty lively place.
>
> A man could be happy there, (*Hymns* 58)

In darkness, he discovers a new light, a new meaning which enshrines the totality of Ezekiel's vision as a poet.

C.D. Narasimhaiah rightly comments:

> Ezekiel has not inherited the great classical tradition of India, of Vedas and Upanishads but to the extent he has availed himself of the composite culture of India to which he belongs, he must be said to be an important poet not merely in Indian context, but in a consideration of those that are writing poetry anywhere in English. (Narasimhaiah 40)

He tries to uphold the significance of the familial bondage. Ezekiel does not defy or idealize the relationships that members of a family share. On the other hand, he depicts it objectively, even at times. Ezekiel has devoted a good number of poems to the apparently trivial problems of family and even to the members of the family. Unlike Ramanujan and Parthasarathy, Ezekiel's use of family as a metaphor is objective in the sense that he does not involve any autobiographical traits in these poems. While Ramanujan and Parthasarathy write about the family with which they are personally involved, Ezekiel views it from a distance, as an inside outsider.

In a good number of poems Ezekiel portrays woman as the protector, the creator, the centre of love under whose fostering care the home gathers significance and meaning. Perhaps, no other Indian poet in English has been successful in portraying the image of a mother as Ezekiel does in "Night of the Scorpion". The poet's mother—the central figure in the poem—is stung by a scorpion in a rainy night. The mother wriggles in pain. The news spreads in the village and the neighbours in a large number rush in. They surround her, uttering god's name, recommending traditional methods of treatment based on innocent faith and superstitions. They exchange their superstitious beliefs; someone arguing that the movement of the scorpion would lead to reciprocal rise of poison in the body of the mother, others suggesting that the poison of the scorpion would burn away the sins of her previous birth and would purify her flesh. Contrary to the rustic, superstitious practices and beliefs of the innocent villagers, the poet portrays the figure of the father as modern and scientific. He is restless too. He uses his 'Powder, mixture, herb' to cure his wife, who wriggles on the mat. She feels quite relaxed when finally the power of the poison subsides. The mother only says:

> Thank God, the scorpion picked on me,
>
> And spared my children. (*The Exact Name*)

This magnanimity, this profoundly human sentiment, this selfless love for the children is what an Indian mother possesses. She is, as it were, the still-point, consuming all the contrary situations of home. The tenderness evoked in the lines is uniquely in harmony with the Indian family. Ezekiel brilliantly records the world of ritualistic incantation when the holy man attempts to tame the poison:

> May she sit still, they said
> May the sins of your previous birth
> be burned away

tonight, they said.
May your suffering decrease
the misfortunes of your next birth, they said
May the sum of evil balanced in this unreal world
against the sum of good
become diminished by your pain.
May the poison purify your flesh
of desire, and your spirit of ambition,
they said, and they sat around
on the floor with my mother in the centre,
the peace of understanding on each face.
(*The Exact Name*)

Ezekiel is in quest of this "peace of understanding" which would make the home an abode of bliss. With ease and precision these lines convey the Indian voice, their simplicity and beliefs as well as their spontaneous human goodwill.

M.K. Naik appreciates the freshness of the poem's theme and the directness of its style:

> It is a poem which only an Indian English poet could have written, since the experience and the responses to it recreated there are rooted in the modern Indian situation. And an art rooted in the soil has freshness and a vigour which no amount of clever pastiche dressed up in sheer technical virtuosity can ever hope to possess. (*Dimensions of Indian English Literature* 36-37)

Ezekiel's purpose in this poem may not be to express sceptism but rather the exact notion of what he observed as a child. The poem shows a new direction, a reality of Indian life particularly emotional Indian mother. Ezekiel tries to show tribute to her.

Rajiv S. Patke has rightly pointed out observing the colonial mindset of the postcolonial poets/writers:

> The postcolonial poets show a marked preference for free verse. They include (1) avoidance of recurrent patterns of stress and syllable, (2) dominance of the image, (3) regulated syntax based loosely on the spoken idiom, (4) linear movement, (5) relatively unobtrusive sound

> structure, and (6) visual presentation on the printed page that is not too different from conventional metered verse, except in its use of variable line length. (Patke 7)

Ezekiel writes free verse, uses certain metrical norms, with an honest, simple clear line. He keeps away from complications, parentheses, oppositions, ellipses, more counter point than melody. He has experimented with from, but never has used typographical dislocations, or a long line stretching to many syllables. He experiments freely with different forms, modifying them suitably to various areas of experience.

'The Railway Clerk' is an important case study of self-definition and self-articulation, when he conveys his helplessness:

> I am never neglecting my responsibility,
>
> I am discharging it properly,
>
> I am doing my duty,
>
> But who is appreciating?
>
> No body. I am telling you. (*Collected Poems* 184)

One may laugh at the language used by the clerk in the poem, but Ezekiel expresses the agony and suffering of the clerk at his workplace truthfully and realistically. Parthasarathy once wrote: 'Language is a tree/loses colour in another sky'. And this is all the more true in India because English has been transformed under the Indian sky. Ezekiel has manipulated the English language to express the way most semi-literate Indians write, speak and perhaps understand.

In the poem 'The Professor' he writes:

> If you are coming again this side by chance,
>
> Visit please my humble residence also,
>
> I am living just an opposite house's backside.
>
> (*Collected Poems* 239)

The professor's description of his house and its location is vague and humorous. But Ezekiel has shown the Indian way of saying things which are circumlocutory in nature.

Irony is the chief weapon Ezekiel uses in his writings to satirize the contemporary society. In one of his poems he suggests to adopt the global trend of family planning in a satirical vein:

These are the days of family planning
I am not against. We have to change with times
Whole world is changing. In India also
We are keeping up. Our progress is progressing
Old values are going, new values are coming
Everything is happening with leaps and bounds.
(*Collected Poems* 239)

Through his poems Ezekiel tries to express the selfishness and hypocrisy of the Professor. Professor Seth has eleven grandchildren, but at the same time he argues for family planning. The frequent use of irony, satire and paradox shows Ezekiel's mastery over the language. His genius lies in his mastery of the colonial language and its skilful manipulation to suit to the Indian content and context.

In 'Servant' Ezekiel presents the acute suffering of a maid-servant and sympathetic attitudes of his mother. He depicts the reality of the social situation in terms of the behaviour of the working class men towards their wives. The maid-servant arrives at the master's house early in the morning for usual domestic work. She happens to be the mother of a child her husband beats her up mercilessly. This reflects of cultural disorientation of the working class. The maid-servant narrates her pitiable story to the mother who consoles her and takes pity on her. The poet takes a humanitarian stance to portray the difference between the two women:

My mother
sees the weal's on back and thighs
provides the ointment over tea and sighs
describes to me what she saw and how these
people are. (Nandy 15)

The plight of the maid-servant in "Ganga" is also distressing. Ganga—the maid-servant—is suspected of prostitution, yet she is not dismissed. The exploitive natures of modern city dwellers are exhibited in this poem. On the other hand:

> She always gets a cup of tea preserved for her
> form the previous evening, and a chapatti, stale
> but in condition. (*Hymns* 37)

Ezekiel's study of domestic problems is meticulous and through it he projects a humanistic view of home and its members. In "The truth about Dhanya", the poet depicts the poverty-stricken condition of Dhanya:

> He cannot
> stand upright
> or walk without pain,
> does odd jobs
> for the ten families
> of The Retreat, collects
> a few coins every day,
> uses them for tea
> and smoking.
> Given food, he eats,

The role of a mother in family is significant in the sense that she embodies in herself the roles of a mentor and a protector. She influences the family by her religious nature. In "Cows" Ezekiel portrays such a mother who believes that cows bear mythic importance, in so far as they serve as the saviour of the dead. But mother gets annoyed with the cows, for they obstruct her mission of collecting money for school:

> She knows
> that cow's holy, worshipped by the parents
> of the children in her school. Even gods ought
> not to clutter up the pavements—that's her view.
> She is not against beliefs: believe what you like.
> She says but get out of my way. She sways and
> smoothly turns, and picks her way from cow to cow
> towards her destination. (Nandy 18)

The mother-figure, as presented above, is the symbol of and educator and protector of society in the expanded family. Her mission of setting up a school is profoundly religious. Ezekiel portrays the mother-figure in his poetry from diverse facets and thus perceives her as central to the framework of an Indian family.

The city, despite its problem becomes Ezekiel's home, his roots. But he is very much critical of the urbanised families which are afflicted by psychic imbalances. In a small poem "Family", Ezekiel presents his critical view on the members of particular family who suffer from some sickness or other. Some suffer from a feeling of being rootless, other in search of a Guru or a God or an Ashram or Gita classes. The sickness is purely psychological. The poet's directness is incisive and it evokes humor because of the tone of informality:

Time is ripe for Saibaba.
Time is ripe for Muktananda.
Let father go to Rajneesh Ashram.
Let mother go to Gita classes.
What we need is mediation.
Need to find our roots, Sir.
All of us are sick, Sir. (*Latter-Day Psalms* 29)

Ezekiel chooses his mild satire by exposing the folly, vices and showy nature of the modern man It may be the need of the hour to maintain good health by doing mediation to control the self.

In "Edinburgh Interludes, Lightly" the poet in a conversational style dramatizes a very common problem of an Indian family i.e. the mother-in-law's pretentious nature and her control over the family and her real disdain for the daughter-in-law. Sometimes the Indian mother apprehends to lose control over her son after his marriage. So she tries to make halla to attract the attention to her son, husband and other members of the family. The statement of the son to his wife is quiet interesting:

She is a very kind woman, you know.
There are not many who do

all the work in the kitchen.
Said the son to his energy bride,
"If you quarrel with my Mother,
you quarrel with me."
That's where the matter stood
when I last heard of it. (*Collected Poems* 291-92)

As the guardian of the family, the father-in-law makes an attempt to bring about harmony in the family. The son, of course, cannot dispense with his loyalty to his parents. Ezekiel ironically brings the poem to a close, leaving to the imagination of the reader the events that might happen after the son's virtual declaration of war against his wife.

In yet another poem "Case Study", Ezekiel investigates the reasons of failure in maintaining harmony and domestic case:

His marriage was the worst mistake of all.
Although he loved his children when they came.
He spoilt them too with just that extra doll,
Or discipline which drove them to the wall.
His wife and changing servants did the same–
A man is damned in that domestic game.
(*The Unfinished Man*)

Such damnation, on the one hand, is a part of the vast panorama of the living reality which Ezekiel shows in this poem.

Ezekiel observes with exactness and frankness the dominating nature of women in educated families even in a male dominated Indian society. He expresses the sheer helplessness of the husband before the dominating wife who wounds him with a number of questions when he comes back home in the evening:

Did you post that letter?
Did you make that telephone call?
Did you pay that bill?
.....
Did you bank that cheque?
Did you by those tickets?

Did you ask if cheese is in stock or not?
(*Latter-Day Psalms* 29)

The innocent, all-enduring husband absorbs all those sour shouting's of his wife, for he knows that if he raises his voice or argues, it would surely create a storm in the family and lead to loss of peace. By employing irony, Ezekiel unravels the core of reality. On the one hand, he tries to present the ethos as it is, while on the other, thorough satiric undertones he reveals his disapproval of these attitudes. The helpless husband only comments:

Shout at me, woman
What else are wives for. (27)

In "The Truth About the Floods" Ezekiel deftly, presents the plight of the villagers affected by flood. The poverty and deplorable plight of the villagers get registered in the following lines:

I have eleven children.
Two I have left to the mercy of God.
The rest are begging, somewhere. (*Hymns* 19)

Ezekiel's dig at poverty gets sharpened as the villager declares "I've eleven children". Another woman narrates her woeful plight:

'I have not eaten for three days.'
'My husband has been washed away.'
'My parents have abandoned me.'
'My son is dying.'
'I cannot find my daughter.' (19)

Even in a critical situation like flood, the woman is deeply concerned about her husband and children. Ezekiel upholds the subtlety of familial relationships. His intention is to glorify the Indian mother/wife. He does not hesitate to expose the corrupt machinery of the government and administration. The affected villagers have developed a bitter attitude towards the government officials who are corrupt and who derelict their duties even at the cost of the suffering masses. Despite their disgust the villagers do not blame any one. They heap all blames on their fate and they believe that "the Nature had conspired against them" (21). Ezekiel shows indirectly the colonial mind set of the Indians which restrain them to claim their own rights in a welfare state.

"Guru" (*Hymns* 25-26) is a biting satire on the hypocritical nature of the saints today. The guru, in this poem, as his past record shows, was a sinner. His present record shows that his ways of living are filthy and foul. He is a 'faithless friend' (26), who is 'obstinate in argument, ungrateful, unkind towards the servants and the poor', 'discourteous to disciples, especially men', 'but he is very much scrupulous in checking/ the accounts of the ashram'. He is fat too. Though the saint possesses all unsaintly qualities, he is popular and commands respect from some people, if not from all. Ezekiel's bitter satire culminates in the concluding interrogation:

> If saints are like this,
> What hope is there then for us? (26)

In 'Poverty Poem' (*Latter-Day Psalms* 13) Ezekiel makes use of irony to expose the reality of the place he lives in. The white woman smilingly offers a coin to a beggar who reciprocates with a smile. Amiable and friendly. Ezekiel dwells entirely on character and scene for a brief sojourn. There is hardly any forward motion in the logical development of character. The secret of an Ezekielian character is exposed towards the conclusion of the poem. His characters are ordinary people, clerks, teachers, section officers, hotel keepers, non-descript customers, self-proclaimed patriots, and the faceless man in the street. Though they are ordinary, they have an unstated dream of becoming/ being someone. Browning's characters are individuals who are extraordinary, that is, they are aristocrats, nobles, artists; they are exceptional ones. Through ordinary characters. Ezekiel tries to convey a sense and a meaning.

Ezekiel is a close observer of the ethos of the place he lives in. His understanding of the problems of society and family is profound. Ezekiel establishes a veritable link with India in general and Bombay in particular. The foregoing discussion of some of Ezekiel's poems makes it convincingly clear that the poet seeks to reaffirm his faith in the place he lives and writes in.

Ezekiel's quest for and his predominant occupation with home gets fully realized through his aesthetic vision. Once the problem of identity is resolved, and the commitment to a place and its ethos is articulated, Ezekiel looks within his self and feels the need to purify the self through self-mockery, and through realization of the deep seated failures embedded in the self.

Ezekiel believes that in a fast-disintegrating world, it is poetry which can bring about coherence and order. Ezekiel not only redefines his identity by approximating his poetry to the language of the people, but legitimizes the significance of an aesthetic vision inherent in the process. Ezekiel is the first Indian poet to use English as an ordinary average Indian speaks. He admits in an interview:

> I use Indian English for comic as well as realistic purposes. As for exploring its dramatic possibilities fully, I certainly would not claim that I have done so. But denigration is always far from my mind. Those who are not touchy about the use of Indian English in literature will of course be suspicious. There is little I can do about that. The important thing for me is that the use of Indian English by some characters should be vindicated by their reality. Such characters exist and that's their way they speak. (Reddy 5-6)

The comic elements presents in his writing shows another dimension which reflects his use of 'Babu-angrezi' his originality. In 'Goodbye Party for Miss Puspa T.S., Ezekiel dramatizes a situation in which the speaker uses present continuous for future in his speech at the farewell meeting for Miss Puspa T.S. who is about to leave for abroad. The comic as well as humorous situation gets reflected throughout the poem the speaker on that occasion begins his farewell speech:

> Friends,
> our dear sister
> is departing for foreign

in two three days,
and/ we are meeting today
to wish her bon voyage. (190)

More interesting is to note that this formal introduction is followed by the speaker's in their compliments to her in the last section of the poem:

Puspa Miss is never saying no
whatever I or anybody is asking
she always saying, yes,
and today she is going
to improve her prospect and we are wishing her bon
voyage. (190)

In other poems like "Patriot", "The Professor", "Irani Restaurant", "Songs to be shouted out", and "Family", Ezekiel makes use of Indian English which is very interesting and humorous. Perhaps writing in this mood would reflect his own identity and our colonial existence. Ezekiel begins as a poet writing poetry in traditional meters and forms. The best examples are "sonnet" and "Love Sonnet", which show his significant achievement and experiment with the speaking voice. "Nudes 1978" is a sequence of 14 sonnets having different structures. Bruce King rightly pointed out that these unrhymed sonnets 'are among Ezekiel's better poem of the latter period' (48). He explores, like a painter of a series of works, the relation between nude and the naked. The process of this transmutation of reality to art is what interests him:

It is not the subject of my love
But a form, as art
In which I am observed. (Warning: Two Sonnets)

Ezekiel's creative mid is in quest of such an order, such a harmony as is in the home. He discovers continuity in life and in poetry. In the 'Foreword' to *Sixty Poems*, Ezekiel maintains that 'there is in each a line or phrase, and idea or image, which helps me to maintain some sort of continuity in my life. 'Karnani in his study of Ezekiel's poetry argues:

> With this noble aim, he treated life as a journey where poetry would be the chief source of discovering and organizing one's self.... An early poem throws light on later on because the poet is under one continuous process of formulating his life in terms of his poetry. (Karnani 14)

J. Birje Patil in trying to relate Ezekiel's poetry to the confessional mode feels that: "The poet himself is the undisguised speaker, the subject-matter is self, and a cross-fertilizing relationship is established between art and the poet's personal life" (Patil 201).

The discovery of such a link between the creative self and poetry and the possibility of ordering the one through the other is crucial for Ezekiel with regard to the evolution of his existential aesthetics. The seed of Ezekiel's quest for home and a perfect self were shown in his early poetry which germinated in the middle of his creative career and finally got fructified in his later poetry.

This discovery of a kinship between poetry, life and world, form the core of Ezekiel's aesthetic vision. V.A. Shahane argues:

> A reading of his poems makes me believe that Ezekiel not quite content with playing the role of a poet, pure and simple, but he is rather fascinated by a wider world, first, there is, the world of poetry and art, and second, there is the larger world of reality and facts.... In Ezekiel the stress in a minor key is almost always on the world of reality. As a result, his poetry suffers as art, though there are various meeting points where his poetry seems happily wedded to his philosophy and his ideas. (Shahane 258)

Even when the poet is physically away from Bombay, he bears within him the seeds of his Bombay existence. He is determined to find out his own room, clean and quiet, in Bombay where he is not a guest but an insider and a native how enjoys freedom and can live with a comforting sense of belonging. Ezekiel's poetry is, thus, a metaphoric journey into the heart of existence, a striving towards the vision of a Home-Bound Pilgrim.

In an early poem "A Poem of Dedication" Ezekiel formulates his poetic creed:

> I don't want the yogi's concentration.
> I do not want the perfect charity

Of saints nor the tyrant's endless power.
I want a human balance humanly
Acquired, fruitful in the common hour. (*Sixty Poems* 3)

Thus it is evident that human relationships, warmth of human bondages become Ezekiel's central concern. His love for commonness intensifies; his vision of life enlarges.

In the poem 'Progress' Ezekiel celebrates human growth. The poem is autobiographical in the sense that it unravels the process of growth in the poet himself.

The study of Ezekiel's poetry would remain incomplete without making a reference to his quest for the spiritual home. In fact, this quest-motif constitutes a veritable part of his identity.

Ezekiel writes to Professor Bogner, as quoted by Shahane:

> I was brought up in a mildly orthodox Jewish home which gradually became Liberal Jewish synagogue, in Bombay until I abandoned religion altogether soon after leaving school. (Shahane 254)

It is relevant in this context to know Ezekiel's personal views on his religious beliefs. 'My religion' Ezekiel wirtes, 'is the religion of a nonreglious man' (Rajangam 4).

Ezekiel tries to come to terms with himself through analysis and introspection. The evolution of his poetry reveals the process of realizing the need for religious commitment or spiritual concern. The pot perceives his own situational crux as dark, temporary and seductive. His willingness to absorb himself in a vision or a moment of illumination has been presented in 'Scriptures' (*Sixty Poems*).

In a small poem 'Healers' Ezekiel expresses his faith in the Master, the creator and in his invisible powers. In every mode of experiencing the problems of life, God's love remains strewn over the individuals:

The Master
Knows the secret. It does not matter
if your marriage is arranged. It does
not matter if you cannot love your wife.

> It does not matter if you teach or
> advertise. God's love remains your heritage. (14)

And every individual retains within himself the capacity to pray and mediate. The poet becomes a prophet, and advises us:

> release your Kundalini
> get your Shakti awakening
> and float with the spirit to your destination. (14)

The poet ennobled by experiences and ordeals of the journey, realizes the limitations of the 'godly' and the 'ungodly'. Markand Paranjape includes him in his analyses of mystical poets and states that "Ezekiel's poetry reveals his primary concern with understanding the meaning of his life and attaining self-realization. Poetry seems to be the means to this goal" (201). In an interview to Ranjit Hoskote Ezekiel remarks:

> 'My poetry has helped me discover my faults and weakness; though always to conquer them.'

Ezekiel poetry, in terms of his quest for spiritual home, registers a progression and a striking transformation. His journey grows from that of an atheist-agnostic to an ardent advocate of the psalms. Though this metaphoric journey to the spiritual home, the poet perceives the truth of this identity, the meaning of his own roots. If for Ramanujan and Parthasarathy, language becomes the medium of identification with their roots, for Ezekiel it is his home, his motherland, and his religion. Literally the poet is back to his roots, and the whole gaunt of Ezekiel's poetry envisages a quest for blood-lies, roots and identity.

Home, family or nation is one of the central metaphors in the post-independence Indian English poetry. And, Ezekiel is the pioneering poet to have strengthened home, family or nation in his poetry in this age of homelessness. He is conscious of the fact that nuclear family is breaking up; human relationship is becoming complex; and traditional family unit is on the verge of failing apart. Perils of love among members of a family scare him, which he knows, is a great loss for the nation. By harping on strong, authenticating human values, Ezekiel's poetry tries to suggest a kind of vision for home and reconstruct it. Ezekiel recaptures the past values by resisting and reliving in the post in his poetry awareness emphasis on familial kinship lies and thrives on the strength and validity of Indian background. His poetry makes a persistent and endeavour to reconstitute home/ nation with value and tradition, concretize the household system and make familial relationship strong and meaningful.

3

Attipat Krishnaswamy Ramanujan

Attipat Krishnaswamy Ramanujan belongs to an orthodox Hindu Brahmin family in Tamil Nadu. Although he nests in the USA as an American citizen, his spirit has never really detached itself from his own country, nativity, home, culture, relations and family. Ramanujan has simply changed his place, not his blood, the place of his birth, his roots. The bulk of his poetry is home/family/nation related and oriented. The poet plunges into his past, remembers the country of his roots and identity. He is, perhaps, the first Indian poet writing in English who exemplifies that it is possible to write poetry in a second language without sacrificing the distinctive socio-cultural consciousness embodied in the first language. His poetry, therefore, reassures the strength of a new literature which retains the seeds of an indigenous tradition.

Rajagopal Parthasarathy rightly remarks:

> I consider this a significant achievement, one almost without a parallel in the history of Indian English verse. Ramanujan has successfully conveyed in English what at its subtlest and incarnational, is locked up in another linguistic tradition. He has, as a result, indicated the directions Indian English verse is likely to take in the future. ("Letter to the Editor" 66)

This chapter attempts to study Ramanujan's poetry in the light of the poet's attitudes and vision which shows his comforting sense of belonging to a native tradition that has shaped and refined his sensibility, and seeks to explore the ways and means which make him feel "I'm a son of the house".

Ramanujan has to his credit three volumes of verse in English: *The Striders* (1966), *Relations* (1971) and *Second Sight* (1986). His *Selected Poems* was published by Oxford University Press, New Delhi in 1976. His first volume of Kannada poems, *Hokkulalli Hoovilla* was published in 1969, and the second, Mattu Itara Padyagalu, came out in 1977. His translations include *The Interior Landscape* (1970) (from classical Tamil), and *Speaking of Siva* (1973) (from Kannada Vacanas).

Ramanujan's attitudes, as revealed in his poetry, remain crystal clear and unambiguous. Often relapsing into his own private past, Ramanujan tries to resolve the problem of his own identity. His poems assert that past is neither a burden nor an imposition on the present, but is profoundly relevant to the individual who has been separated geographically from his own native roots and culture. The willingness to repossess the past and re-enact the past experiences in a world so jejune and rootless becomes Ramanujan's means of understanding his own self in relation to the place and time he chooses to write in. Therefore, Ramanujan, despite his physical distance from India, remains an "instinctive insider", trying persistently to discover the secret solace "in the shade of the family tree" (Daruwalla 24).

Home remains central to the creative process of Ramanujan. It serves as a unifying force that blends individual and tradition, past and present. As Parthasarathy observes, the family, for Ramanujan, is one of the central metaphors with which he thinks ("How It Strikes Contemporary" 189). It is in the metaphor of home that Ramanujan perceives his identity, and frees himself from the agony of an exilic and alienated existence. The poems, in other words, reveal the home-bound vision of Ramanujan.

He himself clarifies his stand thus:

> English and my disciplines (linguistics, anthropology) give me my 'outer' forms—linguistic, metrical, logical and other such ways of shaping experience; and my first thirty years in India, my frequent visits and field trips, my

> personal and professional preoccupations with Kannada, Tamil, the classics and folklore give me my substance, my 'inner' forms, images and symbols. They are continuous with each other, and no longer I can tell what comes from where. (*Ten Twentieth Century Indian Poets* 95-96)

He attempts to achieve a harmony between these two forms. There are three ways in which this harmony is achieved and his sense of being rooted to a native tradition and culture is affirmed.

M.K. Naik, in this context, says:

> This makes for a poetry in which memory plays a vigorous creative role. It is not 'emotion recollected in tranquillity' but recollection emotionalized in tranquil moments that is the driving force behind much of Ramanujan's poetry. ("Echo and Voice" 201)

He tries to define his identity and affirm his vision of and his search for home/nation home-bound pilgrim in a language governed by his Hindu heritage, his racial identity of being a south Indian: "I must seek and will find my particular hell in my Hindu mind" (*The Striders* 32).

Ramanujan's attempt to native English in terms of bringing it closer to classical Tamil and Kannada literature gives his poetry in English certain distinctiveness. Ramanujan incorporates into English a new kind of rhythm and image-formation.

Ramanujan in his note to the interior landscape and love poems from a classical Tamil Anthology (*Kuruntokai*), clearly states the distinctive features of the classical Tamil poetry:

> The Tamil poets had no capitals, punctuation marks, nor any regular end-rhymes in the kind of blank verse they used for all these poems. Tamil, unlike English, has a "free-word-order". The poets make excellent use of their freedom to create their poetic forms; the central nuance of a poem is most often enacted by the unusual yet perfectly acceptable positioning of sentence-parts and by the strategic placing of 'insets' of imagery. (*The Interior Landscape* 11-12)

In 'Afterword', he further makes a classification of Tamil poetry and suggests the reasons for doing so:

> Cankam poetry is classified by theme into two kinds:
>
> Poems of Akam (the inner part or the Interior) and poems of puram (the outer part or the Exterior). Akam poems are love poems; puram poems are all Other kinds of poems, usually about good and evil, action, community, kingdom; it is the 'public poetry' of the ancient Tamils, celebrating the ferocity and Glory of kings, lamenting the death of heroes, the poverty of poets. Elegies, panegyrics, invectives, Poems on war and tragic events are puram poems....
>
> Akam poetry is directly about experience, not action; it is poetry of the 'inner world'. (101-03)

Broadly speaking, Ramanujan's poetry retains the characteristics of Akam poetry. Deployment of technical devices drawn from classical Tamil poetry enables Ramanujan to relate himself to a usable linguistic tradition.

He recollects them and presents them in his poetry with such minuteness of details that one may be tempted to call him a family poet. His poetry reflects a characteristic pattern of beginning with an event or observation in a family relating it to the context of Hindu life or tradition and elevating it to a metaphor or a symbol embodying the problem of his own quest for personal identity (Sreenivasan 112). Ramanujan tries to build up an inscape of his own self-preserving at the bottom the usable memories of his family. The poet paints his father's portrait with a semi-comical undertone in "On the very possible Jaundice of an Unborn Daughter":

> Father sits with the sunflower at the window deep in the yellowing of a revolving chair, fat, bilious, witty, drawing small ellipses in the revolving chair. (*The Striders* 12)

In 'Obituary', Ramanujan dramatizes his encounter with his father's sad, sudden demise. The father has left 'dusty table, 'debts', and 'daughter' (who is considered to be a liability to a Hindu family because of the pervasive practice of dowry system), a 'bed-wetting grandson' (named by toss after him, a cliché of the Hindu family) and 'a house slanting towards the coconut tree'. The father's body burns on the pyre leaving ash for the sons "to pick gingerly/ and throw as the priest/ said, facing east/ where three rivers meet/ near the railway station" (55). The concluding lines of the poem are dismal reminder of the aftermath of the father's death:

> And he left us a changed mother
>
> And more than one annual ritual. (56)

The image of the 'changed mother' illustrates how the catastrophic absence of the husband/father could break the equilibrium of relationship hitherto maintained in the family. Thus 'Obituary' like Ezekiel's 'Night of the Scorpion' highlights the typical ritualistic nuances of a Hindu family. In 'Love poem for wife 1' the poet presents a very humorous portrayal of father's bathing, his marriage dress:

> ....in brothers'
>
> Anecdotes of how noisily father bathed,
>
> Slapping soap on his back;
>
> Find sources for a familiar sheep-mouth
>
> Look in a sepia wedding picture of
>
> Father in a turban. (*Relations* 9)

In "Elements of Composition," Ramanujan consciously and wisely catalogues the constituents of his self. He acknowledges that among many other things he is composed of "father's seed and mother's egg" (*Second Sight* 11).

His father's wisdom makes him understand the agonizing reality around. He remembers his father's words:

> See the cycles, father whispers in
>
> My ear, black holes and white noise,
>
> Elections with four-year shadows,
>
> Red eclipses and the statistics of rape. Connect
>
> Connect, beasts with monks,
>
> Slave economies and the golden bough. (73)

For Ramanujan, as it has been observed, father-figure remains a guide, a beacon of wisdom, a personality who keeps his son vigilant about the slowly degenerating world around him. He clutches and clings on to the memories of father, not merely to ostensibly boast of his lineage, but to suggest that such recollection brings in redemption and security in a totally rootless, faceless existence of the turbulent world.

In Ramanujan's poetry mother occupies a pivotal position, as she does in any Indian family. She is god-fearing, deeply religious, and affection-incarnate. She is the source of goodwill and love. In 'Snakes', the poet, while reflecting on his own fear of snakes, recollects his mother's faith in the religion and the rituals associated with it. He recollects a sacred day when the cobras crawled on the floor of their house:

> The lick the room with their bodies, curves.
> Uncurling, writing a sibilant alphabet
> Of panic on my floor. Mother gives them milk
> In saucers. She watches them such and bare
> The black-line design etched on the brass
> Of the saucer. (*The Striders* 2)

In 'Still Another for Mother', Ramanujan successfully dramatizes a situation in which the man-woman relationship gets into an informal bondage and time affects this bondage mercilessly. Watching the couple behave abnormally—because of the impact of age on them—the poet is reminded of his own mother—and the slow process of time eating away her dowry. The poet painfully concludes the poem with a striking analogy:

> Something opened in the past and I heard
> Something shut in the future, quietly,
> Like the heavy door of my mother's
> Black-pillared, nineteenth century
> Silent house, given on her marriage
> Day to my father, for a dowry. (*The Striders* 14)

The "twisted black bone tree" (5) reminds the poet of his mother's youth. He visualizes how his mother was busy and active, running back from "rain to the crying cradles" (5). In "Ecology" the poet reflects on the mother's innocent love for nature, trees and her immaculate devotion to gods. She would not allow any one to cut the red champak trees, thus, unknowingly, not allowing to distort the ecological balance. The mother, for the poet, lives on for ever in his memory. Even after her death, the mother's affection is not affected or erased.

In Ramanujan's poems, the wife-figure also appears prominently. He catalogues the unique moments of tiff and the residual harmony after the tiff is over. He presents the subtle difference between himself and his wife, between any husband and any wife for that matter. The poet objectively analyses the relationship and begins his poem 'Love poem for wife 1':

> I envy you your village dog-ride
>
> And the mythology
>
> Of the seven crazy aunts. (*Relations* 9)

The poem unfolds the poet's relationship with his father-in-law, and his sister-in-law. He does not hesitate to present the petty-wages, fights that took place between brothers and sisters. In 'Love poem for wife 2' Ramanujan harps on the mystery that exists in the husband-wife relationship. Though it embodies love, care affection and satisfaction, it does not rule out the possibility of quarrels, misunderstandings. In 'Love poem for wife and her trees', written two decades after the two earlier love poems on wife, the poet celebrates the same difference between himself and his wife, between his sensibility and his wife's. the poem illustrates how Ramanujan can dramatize his sense of exile while at the same time assert his commitment to his native roots.

Although Ramanujan is physically distanced from his native land India, he persistently and wholeheartedly makes in an attempt to discover a secret solace in the shades of the family tree. His poetic world is peopled by brothers, sisters, cousins, aunts, and uncles. It is a world dominated by a delicate and invisible bondage of familial love. The touchstone of love governs every insider, every member of joint family. In these family poems Ramanujan tries to emphasize this unit flourishing under the aegis of the family brings comfort, solace and satisfaction of being rooted and home-bound.

He innocently believed that his sister's braid had scales. Sometimes, the poet exposes the peculiarities of his sisters. His description creates humour:

> Our sisters were of various sizes,
> one was ripe for a husband and we
> were not poor. (*The Striders* 7)

When his sisters go to the market, she become busy with many trifle things. Sometimes they purchase certain items for the household, and find pleasure in gossiping with a buyer. The poet details their activities and attitudes humorously:

> They often stopped: may be for a chat
> With a buyer, or a dip into patchwork
> Pouches for betel nut and tobacco, or
> Likelier still, to lay a little
> Silver nest-egg under the mat to
> Hatch on a rainy day.

Sometimes the poet, accompanied by his sister, cherishes strange hopes quite natural to children:

> My sister and I have always wished a tree
> Could shriek or at least writhe
> Like that other snake we saw under the
> Break of the crow. (8)

In 'Looking for a cousin on a Swing' Ramanujan portrays the difference between the cousin's childhood fancy of swimming with another cousin and her present youthful plight of searching for a swing in the cities. The poet quite interestingly observes the change that has overtaken his cousin:

> Now she looks for the swing
> In cities with fifteen suburbs
> And tries to be innocent about it. (17)

There is still another cousin who can make the air resonant with her cries:

Mention any cousin's death in the
Walled red-fort city: she will weep
Aloud with no thought of neighbours. (37)

The poet recollects the cousin playing on the swing, with his sister. He portrays his sister as "cool porcelain" (*Second Sight* 29), and his little aunt wearing a stone face. By so doing the Poet proves himself to be an expert reporter of his family and familial ties and bondages.

Apart from portraying his father, mother, uncle, aunt, brother, sister and relations, Ramanujan has also written an number of poems involving all the members of family. Such poems choose to anchor on a specific situation and then move on to describe one member after another of the family in a fascinating manner. Vrinda Nabar while reviewing Ramanujan's selected poems makes an interesting observation:

> Ramanujan's anecdotes, his references to childhood episodes and recollections, are narratives. He picks on the essential image and achieves a social commentary through it. (Nabar 545)

Ramanujan's poetry reveals the secret mechanism with which an Indian joint family operates. He not only unfolds the operational strategy at the emotional and rational levels, but at the spiritual level too. William Walsh makes an interesting observation when he remarks:

> His poems on relatives and insects, on grannies and aunts, on wives and uncles, on the life of the Hindu, show both his devotion to the intense and diminutive, and his sense of the complicated cargo carried by the family relationships. ("Small Scale Observations" 118)

Ramanujan's 'Small-scale Reflection on a Great House' is a classic insofar as it celebrates the specific physiognomy of the Great House that had fostered the growth of his own personality. Ramanujan incorporates into this poem, as well as in others, the neutrality of language, the conscious distancing of the subjective self, the subtle handling of irony as a mode of perceiving reality around—all that he has learnt and inherited from the classical

Tamil and Kannada poetry. Ramanujan images forth the all-pervasive possessiveness of the Great House.

> ...nothing
> That ever comes into this house goes out.
> Things come in everyday to lose themselves
> Among other things lost long ago among
> Other things lost long ago. (*Relations* 40)

Ramanujan's narrative skill for smug details creates humour:

> Nothing stays out daughters get married
> to short-lived idiots; sons who run away
> come back in grandchildren who recite Sanskrit
> To approving old men, or bring betel nuts
> for visiting uncles who kept them gaping
> with anecdotes of unseen fathers, or to
> bring Ganges water in a copper pot for
> the last of the dying ancestors'
> rattle in the throat. (42-43)

The tone of the poem is homogenous, except towards the end where it changes from humorous to serious and tragic.

'History' unfolds yet another layer of family history. The poem moves round the event of the poet's great aunt's death. In the process of unfolding, and the poet hints at the selfishness and narrowness of the 'petite little dark aunt' and other aunts. The poet as a child did not miss the chance of watching how his great-aunt was 'laid out, face incurious/ eyes yet unshut' (51). The poet does not; of course directly tell us about the selfishness of his aunt. His aunts started cleaning the body of the grand-aunt before she was cold. They removed diamond ear-rings. Bangles, anklets, hair-pins and toe-rings from her body, not as a token of memory of the dead, but as real addition to their wealth.

The poet's narrative reveals the nature of the aunts:

> Her two
> Daughters one dark one fair,
> Unknown each to the other alternately

Picked their mother's body clean
Before it was cold, or the eyes were shut,
Of diamond ear-rings, bangles, anklets
The pin in the hair, the toe-rings from
Her wedding the previous century, all
Except the gold in her teeth and silver string....
(*Relations* 52)

The selfishness of the little aunt was moved by the death of the great aunt. She wept into tears. This reciprocity of tears and love between members of joint-family is highlighted to reiterate Ramanujan's unflinching faith in the traditional familial ties.

In 'Extended Family', Ramanujan tries to relate himself to other members of his family in terms of showing liken likeness of his habits and attitudes with those others. He bathes like his grandfather at the village well. He 'slaps' sop on his back like his father. He listens to 'faint morning songs' like his mother.

What Ramanujan intends to celebrate in these family poems is not euphoristic, egoistic lineage of his own identity, but his indebtedness and allegiance to the tradition. For Ramanujan, past matters as much as the present. Placed against an alien culture, his memories of childhood serve as a positive reminder of his origin, his roots. This implicit awareness of one's origin is redemptive in so far as it protects one form the loss of face or identity. Family, renders psychological sustenance and security to an exile. It is through the metaphor of family and centrality of home in Ramanujan's consciousness that he tries to relate himself to India.

The poet is deeply aware of his Hindu Brahminical Background. He uses irony as a mode of exploring the Hindu psyche. Dramatizing through anecdotes and incidents, the poet is able to dive deep into the exact nature of the Hindu mid grounded and reared by the Gita, which is on the based culture of his origin. Ramanujan is a Hindu, a modern Hindu whose 'outer' being is influenced by the Western education. He, therefore, does not tend to glorify Hinduism. He is not a rigid and orthodox Hindu who abides by the principles and ethics coded in the Gita and other traditional scriptures. He is not even elated at the fact that he is a Hindu. Withdrawing himself to a distance, he tries to study and analyses the exact nature of a Hindu mind.

William Walsh rightly observes Ramanujan's distinction as an Indian poet:

> Ramanujan, an expatriate academic Who works on eastern linguistics, is', unlike Ezekiel, deeply possessed of or by, the Indian ethos and psyche in its pure Hindu form. ('Small-scale Observations' 11)

Irony, as a mode of expression and experiencing reality, fascinates Ramanujan not because it serves as a decorative.

Apart from irony, what is significant in this group of poems is the tone of his voice. Parthasarathy appropriates his arguments on the importance of this tone of voice which is Ramanujan's distinction as he writes:

> What sets Ramanujan apart from other poets is his unique tone of voice, a feature that accounts for the characteristic style of his poetry. Tone, therefore, expresses the speaker's attitude towards his subject and towards his audience and sometimes towards himself. The person who is speaking takes into account the particular situation, and the situation determines how the thing is to said. As in speech, so too in poetry, tone is an important factor. ("How It Strikes Contemporary" 196)

In 'A Hindu to his Body' Ramanujan harps on the Hindu concept of the body through the metaphor of a tree. If the family tree stand erect on the earth with its roots deep in the soil, the tree of body is topsy-turvy. The pious Hindus believe that the human body is like a tree upside down, whose roots are in the heaven and whose branches and head are on the earth. In 'the Hindoo: He does not Hurt a Fly or a Spider either' Ramanujan's handling of irony is superb. He tries to dramatize the internal tensions of a Hindu in relation to his god-fearing temperament. As an honest Hindu, the poet does not hurt a fly or a spider for he believes in the theory of Karma and rebirth and in the life after death.

However, Ramanujan's irony in dramatizing the entire situation becomes explicit towards the close of the poem. The Hindoo cannot hurt a fly or a spider, but can forcibly drag a woman to the net of his love. Relating personal relationships to the matters of religious conviction, Ramanujan tries to mock at the shallowness of the gentle gesture of a Hindu. When the poet writes that the Hindoo reads his Gita and is calm at all events', he ironically harps on the duplicities of the Hindoo mind. As a perfect Hindu the poet has learnt to show his equanimity to both good and evil. He even remains calm when "knives, bombs, scandal, and cow dung" (23), fall on women. He watches lovers without envy, but carefully watches the houseflies rubbing their legs or kissing. The poet highlights the hypocrisy hidden in the Hindu mind.

In "The Hindoo the only Risk" Ramanujan has become all the more explicit in showing the cross-section of a Hindu heart wherein lies the heartlessness. The poet explores through a series of visual images how risky it is to be a Hindu. He tries to quiet down his heartbeat at the "neighbour's striptease" or a "friend's suicide" (34). He is selfish to the extent of being meticulous about "three square meals at regular hours". The poet christens this attitude of the Hindu as a "bottomless enterprise" (34). Thus prompting his eagerness to reconstruct his culture and religion that have been debased and degraded.

"Prayers to Lord Murugan", Ramanujan's much discussed poem written in the light of classical Tamil forms, aptly "satirizes the cultural complacency" of the Hindus (Nabar 546). In an interview with Ramnath Jha, Ramanujan admits with humility his deep-rooted allegiance to the Tamil forms.

> My poem "Murugan" for instance,
> Could not have been written if I
> Did not know classical Tamil forms
> And even some of the images there. (Jha 7)

He admits:

> I prefer the classical. A typical 'Sangam' poem
> Has a well-defined, well-wrought complex form. It

Has an articulate body of convention behind it.
The image is not flaunted here but is sharp and
Pointed. (Nakalan 11)

The eleven prayers that make the poem try to juxtapose imagery drawn from tribal life, a life that revolves in tune with nature, and the sophisticated shallow urban life that is mechanical, parasitical, embedded in by pretensions and fabrications. Prayer usually is a means of cleansing oneself of vices, sins, guilt, which drag a man (Hindu) towards the dark region of the Hell. Through prayer, a Hindu mind tries to establish rapport with the Divine, illumine the darkness within, and finally reaches the still centre of the eternal abode.

However, these prayers do not ennoble us, nor do they inspire humility in us; rather they intensify the pettiness, the meanness, the shallowness and the rottenness of an egocentric island existence in a spiritually bankrupt world, lord Murugan is the 'ancient Dravidian god of fertility, joy, youth, beauty, war and love. He is presented as a six-faced god with twelve hands" (*Relations* 57). Ramanujan in the first section of the poem expresses his deep sense of loss because Lord Murugan, like the river Vaikai, has lost significance in a spiritually bankrupt world. The rituals associated with the worship of the lord no longer purify the hearts of the people. The poet laments on this loss:

O where are the cockscombs and where
The beaks glinting with new knives
At cross roads/ when will orange banners burn/
Among blue trumpet flowers and shade
Of trees/ waiting for lightening? (*Relations* 57)

The poet reiterates the pettiness of modern man who can eat away his own past, and rely wholeheartedly on his own enclaved existence in the present.

Lord of headlines
Help us read/ the small print. (61)

Or

Deliver us O presence
From proxies/ and absences
From Sanskrit and the mythologies
Of night.... (61)

Or

Lord, return us,
Bring us back to a litter
Of six new pigs in a slum
And a sudden quarter of harvest.

The concluding prayer reaches the zenith of irony:

Lord of lost travellers
Find us. Hund us down.
Lord of answers cure us at
Once of prayers. (62)

The concluding prayer is a deliberate play of irony, and it has created confusion in the minds of some who feel that Ramanujan does not believe in Lord Murugan. Nissim Ezekiel trying to locate the Indianness of Indo-English poetry in general and Ramanujan's poetry in particular, observers:

> Paradoxically, the 'Prayers to Lord Murugan'
> Which promise a wholly Indian ethos remind
> Us that Ramanujan does not believe in Lord
> Murugan or any other Hindu god. Lord Murugan
> Is asked at the end of the sequence to 'cure
> Us at once of prayers' which can hardly be
> Termed an Indian prayer. ("What is Indian" 52)

Ramanujan has expressed his prayers, at certain places, with sincerity and honesty and devotion. For mischance:

Lord of faces find us the face
We lost early this morning. (*Relations* 60)

Or

Lord of solutions, teach us to
Dissolve and not to drown. (61)

Or

Lord of the last-born give us birth. (62)

Or

Lord of answer cure us at once of prayers. (62)

These prayers, viewed from a modernized perspective, seem to be genuine and sincere. The poet through these prayers tries to cleanse and purify himself from the prevailing pettiness of existence in a mechanical, culturally and spiritually derailed world, he tries to relate himself to the centre of his native existence where there is harmony between nature and man and thus with god.

'A Minor Sacrifice' is yet another interesting episodic poem that weaves fabrics of family and Hindu faith. The poem is in five sections, and each section perpetuates the progression of the narrative with such intensity that the boundaries between the epic and the real disappears. The poem begins with a reference to the story of an epic. A mischievous king killed a snake and garlanded a saint with the dead snake. The saint was angry and cursed the king who died early of a snakebite. His son promised to take revenge. He arranged an altar and performed sacrifice and magical rites. Snakes from everywhere of all varieties were magically charmed to fall on the altar and all the snakes were burnt to death. This episode from the epic serves as the background to the poem.

Ramanujan interestingly reveals the peculiarities of the Hindu culture and the typical traditional nuances of the Hindu psyche in his poetry. But the tone with which he makes such revelation does not suggest his willingness either to praise it or to detest it. His ironic mode of viewing reality makes him accept the world within and without as it is. This attitude, this willing acceptance of things as they are, determines Ramanujan's modernist sensibility.

S.K. Desai mistakes the poet's intentions when he says:

> Through memories he is not seeking his roots (in the area of darkness), nor is he exploring the wounded or healthy Hindu civilization. He is using them simply to explore the existential problems of time and what it does to life. (Desai 117)

Memory, in fact, has a therapeutic effect on the poet's highly mechanized existence in an alien city.

G.N. Devy rightly maintains:

> Whenever he faces the problem of the loss of identity he turns back to his family identity. All branches of his existence can be traced back to one seed—the family. (Devy 11)

The flux-fixity existential dilemmas lead the poet to take shelter under the aegis of the family tree. Therefore, home that enshrines family becomes the central metaphor of Ramanujan's consciousness and he makes a writing and deliberate effort to reconstruct home by clinging on to his family, his native land and his roots and its culture, religion and heritage.

What Ramanujan successfully achieves at the end of his journey in relation to the poems discussed here—is the discovery of his own self, its identity in relation to his roots and family and home. In the process of this discovery, he has tried to revitalize the past to show us the home-bound vision such a home-bound vision emerges from the poet's inner compulsion to cling to his Tamil roots and his instinctive awareness of the centrality of familial experiences.

Ramanujan's reliance on the memory of his own Indian past as the saving shield against the mounting sense of alienation and insecurity, his insistence on the assimilation of the classical linguistic traditions and the creative use of English in order to give Indian poetry in English a definite identity, an indigenous flavours make him an instinctive insider. Although Ramanujan is caught in the cross-currents of two cultures—the Indian and the American—he always writes with a Tamil sensibility. He writes his poetry in an idiom that is shaped and rounded by nativized sensibility and home-bound vision. English is Ramanujan's adopted language, the second language, and though he writes his poetry in his adopted second language, he never sacrifices the distinctive socio-cultural consciousness that his first native language embodies. In fact, he uses English language for outer forms and discipline and also as a subsitution of post-colonialism in Indian.

4

Rajagopal Parthasarathy

Rajagopal Parthasarathy, a significant contemporary Indian poet, evolved an indigenous tradition in Indian English poetry by returning to his native linguistic tradition. He was the first Indian English poet to switch over to Tamil as his creative medium and acclimatize English poet to switch over to Tamil as his creative medium and acclimatize English language to his native tradition. Born in a conservative Brahmin family in Tamil Nadu, although he migrated and stayed abroad with a Western lifestyle, Parthasarathy has constantly been observed with his native heritage and culture. His initial infatuation for and flirting with the colonial language ended up in a disaster with the dawning of a deeper realization of his loss of roots consequent upon the British rule on the Indians. Caught in the cross currents of two cultures—the Indian and the Western colonial—he gradually got disenchanted with the latter. The poet's growing disenchantment had him realize the significance of his own roots, his native culture and tradition.

Quest for home is the quest for being rooted; it is a continuous process in post-independence Indian poetry. Parthasarathy's poetry not only explores the image of home/family, society/nation, it also tries to make a journey back to home by ennobling and glorifying the values embedded in it. The present chapter attempts to study the poetry of Rajagopal Parthasarathy in the light of his native Tamil tradition and identify his own roots, culture and heritage with a deep sense of belonging and familial relationship, which, the poet realizes, are the stepping stones for construction of home/nation. Born in Tiruchirapalli, Tamil Nadu in 1934, Parthasarathy began to learn English at the age of ten in Don BOSCO Father's School, and studied at Siddhartha College, Mumbai and at Leeds University, U.K. where he was British Council scholar in 1963-64. He was a Lecturer in English Literature in Mumbai between 1959 and 1971 before joining Oxford University Press in 1971 as Regional Editor in Madras. He is Associate Professor of English and Asian Studies at Skidmore College in Saratoga Springs, New York, USA. Parthasarathy edited *Ten Twentieth-Century Indian Poets* published by Oxford University Press in 1976. His translation into Modern English Verse of the 5th century Tamil epic, *'Cilappatikaram' of Hanko Atikal* (*The Tale of an Anklet*)—an Epic of South India composed 1500 years ago was published by Columbia University Press, USA, in 1993 won him the prestigious PEN Literary Award in 1994. He was a member of the University of Iowa writing program during 1978-79. Like the most colonized Indian minds, he dreamt of England as his future home and the English language as the strongest link to have a sense of belonging there. The English education made so deep and early impression on him that he became critical about everything in India.

As he states:

> And exposed as I was to English ideas and attitudes, I became hypercritical of everything Indian. Indian society was, I felt, deeply neurotic, its feet chained to a grossly exaggerated past. There was, again, something terribly wrong with the Indian character itself. Spiritually bankrupt and powerless to absorb the shocks of twentieth century, Indian was a 'nation of sleep-walkers,' its people sick in the mind and helpless. The nation had, kept telling myself, lost its will to live. (Parthasarathy 1982: 66)

Like all colonized mindset, Parthasarathy too looked upon England as the most productive land and English language as the most viable medium to make him a celebrity writer. So he chose England as his future abode. However, his dating with England/English became traumatic in course of time, which not only shattered his dreams but also gave him a culture shock. He soon realized that contemporary England was no less imperialistic towards India and the Indians even after the end of their colonial rule here. He looked at his own plight critically at an alien land and an alien culture and felt an urgent need to redefine and authenticate his own self, his identity in relation to his own culture and native land, his roots, *Rough Passage*, Parthasarathy's single volume of verse, which embodies twenty years of writing speaks of the growth of the poet's mind and serves as a brilliant record of his quest for the truth about the self.

In *Rough Passage*, the poet initiates a dialogue between himself and his Tamil past. He makes an effort to nativise the alien English language to redefine, and reaffirm his faith in the roots of his native tradition. The poet is caught in the labyrinths of colonialism constructed by the language, but ironically, he uses the same language as a means of freeing himself (Trivedi 48). *Rough Passage* is a three-tier poem divided into 3 parts, 'Exile', 'Train' and 'Homecoming'. Each part is a manifestation of the poet's tension in the journey of his life. The poem is composed in thirty-seven sequences. The dominant voice in each part consists of a dialogue, between the poet and his inner self. These divisions are formal rather that organic as Parthasarathy stresses in his preface that "it should be considered and read as one poem". The poet integrates the three parts by writing the poem in his favourite triplet-stanzas, linking stanza to stanza and sequences to sequences, which givers *Rough Passage* as sense of continuity. The unity thus achieved has the effect of creating the movement of unfolding a consciousness.

Parthasarathy's *Rough Passage* is a significant landmark in the annals of Indian English poetry as it devises an indigenous tradition by way of "innovating and moulding the English language to native ends" (Bhagat 131). Parthasarathy incorporates into the fabric of his poetry certain devices which he has learnt from Tamil poetry. He admits:

> It is closer in style and content to Tamil poetry, especially in its use of irony for deflating the pride of the Tamil in their euphuistic past. ("Introduction and Notes" 4)

In *Rough Passage*, Parthasarathy assimilates his ideas, thoughts and vision and the peculiar nuances of Tamil language with the English language he choose to write in. The primary motif of *Rough Passage* is the discovery of the self and its relation to the roots, home/nation. Parthasarathy's intense sense of alienation and rootlessness made him obsessed with his native heritage, his home and nation, which singularly provides unity to his poems. His quest for home is the reflection of his quest for roots. This quest is perpetuated with honesty, and meditative intensity, because home, for Parthasarathy, is a repository of comfort, security, solace and strength that can appease his ascending tensions. Thus the centrality of the home impels the poet to reach the heights of perfection in terms of ordering words with a view to affirming his vision of rebuilding home/nation. Parthasarathy considers that his journey is suggestive of a movement from the state of ignorance to the state of bliss.

However, in the beginning of his journey the poet is poignantly aware of his disenchantment with his own place, with his own native language. But at the end of his journey, he comes to terms with the place of his nativity and its language without any obvious forebodings or complaints. *Rough Passage* is a saga of the psychic adventure of the self in highly innovative stylistic patterns, and it may be called the return of the native to the epicentre of his home, culture and heritage.

There are altogether eight poems in the 'Exile' section of the *Rough Passage*. Each poem reflects the speaker's intense sense of alienation, and loss of identity. 'Exile-1' introduces the speakers' age, i.e. thirty, and his wisdom of 'refusing' to accept his own image, thereby harping on the crisis of identity, when the poem opens, the poet gives a good look at himself. "At thirty the mud will have settled." He feels responsive to retrospection. It is a process of encounter with the exile:

> As a man approaches thirty he may
> Take stock of himself
> Not that anything important happens.
> At thirty the mud will have settled:

You see yourself in a mirror
Perhaps, refuse the image as yours. (13)

Here the narrator perceives himself as confused with regard to his own image.

'Exile 2' delineates the speaker's sense of exile in the alien land. It is also an idea and a generalization, both of which feed on his sensibility. This verbal mechanism enables the poet, through the persona, to depict his cultural inheritance in terms of a man returning to his lover.

He says:

All night your hand has rested
on her left breast,
in the morning when she is gone
you will be alone like the stone benches
in the park, and would have forgotten
her whispers in the noises of the city. (15-16)

the image of the hand resting on his beloved's breast evokes a number of extremely personal and intimate associations. The sense of security and closeness is vividly realized in this image. 'Noises of the city' bury the speaker's sense of security on the lap of his beloved and posit in him the pangs of alienation that finally reduce him to the lonesome 'stone benches'.

'Exile 2' intensifies the speaker's sense of exile and alienation through his experiences in the 'basement flat' where the pendulum of conversation had swung between two, Ravi Shankar, the maestero of the oriental classical music, and 'cigarette stubs', 'empty bottles' representing the hollowness of western culture. The poet's acute sense of being an exile is further intensified:

Through holes in a wall, as it were,
Lamps burned in the fog
In a basement flat, conversation
Filled the night, while Ravi Shankar,
Cigarette stubs, empty bottles of stout
And crisps provided the necessary pauses.

> He had spent his youth whoring
> after English Gods.
> There is something to be said for exile. (15)

The use of appropriate idioms in a veiled irony in these lines demonstrates the confessional honesty of the poet. One who 'spent his youth whoring after English Gods' is not merely an exile but an embodiment of existential guilt and self-deception (Trivedi 51).

'Exile 3' further precipitates the exiled speaker's uneasiness. When he arrives at his own native city, he is disillusioned too.

For him:

> The streets are noisy. And trees
> On Malabar Hill blind with dust.
> spring had gone unnoticed
> except for the fountains of colour
> in the park.
> Like a hand at rest, the pelagic city
> is immobile. (*Rough Passage* 19-20)

In 'Exile 4', the poet confesses his foolishness of quarrelling with his own city. In spite of his rising sense of uneasiness in the 'hard embrace' of the streets, in it traffic or regulated/affections, 'uneventful' (21), the poet welcomes his retrun, as if, in some unimaginable corner of his mind, there sleeps supinely the contentment and satisfaction of being here in his own home. The poet's realization of the sense of exile comes to full circle, as he finds no difference between his foster land London and his native land Madras.

Even in his own place he feels alienated:

> The city reels under the heavy load
> of smoke. Its rickety legs break
> wind, pneumatically of course in the
> press of traffic. (22)

He is further dismayed at the sight of a cow that 'stands/ in the middle combing traffic' (2). The poets mind gets heavy with clouds of uncertainties about himself and his own roots. He strolls seaward with a view to smothering away his suffering and releases his tension. However, it is the speaker's mounting sense of alienation and rootlessness that provides unity to the poems in the 'Exile' section.

The 'Trial' consists of fifteen small poems. This section typifies the poets attempt to overcome the feelings of exile, alienation and uprootedness through love and responsibilities that begin with marriage (King 240). The 'Trial' opens with the poet in the exalted company of his lady-love trying to acquire 'unspeakable relief'. He shares the lady-love's childhood experiences while paging through the album. He makes an imaginative leap into the loneliness of his lady-love at the moment of her father's sad demise.

The poet then willingly indulges in the trails of flesh in the act of love. Through sharp, precise itemized unpacking of the body's sputter, he tries to justify his sojourn such a long way from Fort St George to the city of Job Charlock. And through such unveiling of the erotic experiences, the poet prepares himself to overcome the overwhelming sense of exile within:

> A nipple hardens
> On the tongue. Here
> Pleasure is elliptic, wholesome. (35)
>
> Or
>
> My hands fill up, slowly,
> With your breasts. (38)
>
> Or
>
> Our bodies scrape home
> For passions, older
> Than the stones of Konark. (38)
>
> Or
>
> The sweet water of your flesh
> I draw with my arms as from a well
> Its taste as ever as on the night
> Of Capricorn. (39)

He has learnt that nothing is permanent, neither the sputter of body, nor the citadel of love. He has ascended many stairs of flesh, dearly held many rails of bones but all in vain, no more than 'the chill promise of a home' (44). He realizes that 'Only/ the heart is not hospitable anywhere' (44). While the places heave betrayals, the words would not, because of 'their unmentionable odour' (45). The poet's realization is total now:

> My past is an unperfected stone:
>
> The flaws show. I polish
>
> The stone sharpen the luster to a point. (45)

The 'Trial' section of *Rough Passage* is both a departure from and a perpetuation of the 'Exile'. It is a departure in the sense that the poet handles the language with no explicit reverberations. He uses the language and exploits its nuances with certain exclusiveness and inwardness to posit in it the vision of a pilgrim determined and destined to rediscover his sanctuary, his home. The poet makes use of dead metaphors and clichés so as to grab his experiences without failing to achieve the necessary indigenousness.

Bruce King makes an interesting observation of metaphors and clinches:

> "Over the family album, 'the other night', 'in the distance, school was a pretty kittle of fish', 'slaked your thirst', 'Hand on chin', 'turned the corner', 'Mortal as I am', 'I have not the key to unlock His gates', 'the heavy lens of non', 'sleeved in a childhood', 'The sweet water/ of your flesh I draw', 'a small hand will do', 'And words, surely, are no more than ripples/ in the deep well of the throat'" (King 240)—all these innovative usages make this section different.

Parthasarathy's deft use of imagery in the 'Trial' section makes it different from the 'Exile' section as it overcomes the dreariness and bleakness of the imagery used in the section of 'Exile'. The 'Exile' section could not sustain a sense of relief, whereas 'Trial' builds it up and looks forward to 'Homecoming', so far as the journey-motif and the vision of the speaker-pilgrim is concerned. 'Trial' retains the thrust handed down by 'Exile'.

'Homecoming' is enriched by the Poet's falling back on his childhood experiences. What, in fact, strengthens his bondage with his roots and facilitates an easy homecoming is the use of language. Experiences in the childhood become significant and memorable and meaningful not because they happened or existed, but because they had been printed boldly in the psyche by the native language or mother tongue. As a modern poet in the postcolonial era, Parthasarathy realized that he must invent for himself an idiom and a medium by clinging to his original linguistic roots.

In fact, the tenor of *Rough Passage* is explicit: to initiate a dialogue between the poet and his Tamil past, "Homecoming", as Parthasarathy admits, tries to derive its sustenance from grafting itself on to whatever I find usable in Tamil tradition—from the Kural (3rd and 4th century A.D.) to Nalayiradivyaprapantam (5th and 9th century) something that had eluded me over the years, I was eventually able to nativise it in English—the flavour, the essence of Tamil mores ("Tradition and Freedom" 54).

The poet's arrival at home—both at linguistic and at metalinguistic level—is explicit in the first poem of 'Homecoming' section:

> My tongue in English chains,
> I return, after a generation, to you.
> I am at the end
> Of my Dravidic tether,
> Hunger for you unassuaged.
> I father, stumble.
> Speak a tried language
> Wrenched from its sleep in the Kural,
> Teeth, palate, lips still new
> To its agglutinative touch.
> Now, hooked on celluloid, you reel
> Down plush corridors. (49)

This 'home-coming' from an illusory 'whoring after English gods' is significant and meaningful in the sense that it manifests in itself the foolishness and impenitence of the poet for remaining away from the agglutinative touch of Tamil. The irony is that he speaks 'a tried language' (49), a language that has become, 'today an unrecognizable carcass' (50).

The poet's 'return' to his home, his roots is significant because he realizes that it is his responsibility as a part of his native linguistic tradition to save it from sterility and decay. He feels it his responsibility to purify the dialect of his tribe.

He asserts:

> The homecoming is therefore, a peculiar return, for what strikes him most as a poet seeking a native mode for creative fulfilment, is the linguist sterility.... Rough Passage is in this sense a departure from the usual stance perceptible in contemporary Indian Poetry in English—for it suggests that the discovery of cultural roots is inextricably linked not only with the choice on one's own language but also with the corresponding responsibility as a creative writer, of cleansing the language of the tribe. (Sivaramkrishna 116)

His home-coming further posits a conviction that foreign poets can no longer become the model for an Indian writer. He has, to 'turn inward' and 'scrape the bottom of his past,' and this is how he can shape the tradition of an indigenous writing. Such a realization is the manifestation of the poet's home-bound vision:

> Turn inward. Scrape the bottom of your past.
> Ransack the cupboard for skeletons
> of your Brahmin childhood
> (the nights with Father's droning
> The Four Thousand as sleep
> pinched your things blue). You may then,
> perhaps, strike out a line for yourself
> from the iron of life's ordinariness. (50)

He therefore, turns inward, 'ransacks the cupboard' of his past familial experiences. He clings to one thread of memory and another and makes an attempt to assuage the wounds experienced in 'Exile' and 'Trial'. 'Homecoming' introduces through a series of visual images, the poet's recollection of a 'family reunion'. He presents the glimpses of Tamil mores and manners, filling our mind with clear experiences and ecstasies of the harmony with splashes of Tamil life:

> This year, Cousins arrived in Tiruchechanur
> in overcrowded private buses
> the dust of unlettered years
> Later, each one pulled,
> sitting cross-legged on the step:
> of the Choultry, familiar coconuts
> out of the fire
> of rice-and-pickle afternoons.
> Sundari, who had squirreled up and down
> forbidden tamarind trees in her long skirt
> every morning with me. (49)

'Cousins started arriving in Tiruchechanur in overcrowded private buses'. They sat 'cross-legged' on the steps of the choultry, enjoying the 'rice-and-pickle' afternoon. The poet saw Sundari, one of his cousins, surrounded by her three daughters. The present moment of the family reunion carries him back to forty years when Sundari used to move up and down the 'forbidden tamarind trees' in her long skirt. The poet, through such a re-collective mode, tries to suggest the significance of such unions. It is the family union which show how deep is the bondage between one member and the other. Only by turning inward towards one's own past that one would be able to anchor oneself in the flowing tradition and would discover one's own roots.

Parthasarathy looks at the past critically, yet affectionately. He recognizes and uses the past as a mode of recreating the present, and he treats it as a part of the grand flow of the tradition he belongs to. Parthasarathy's initial discontent at the present scenario of his homeland is due to the changes and uncertainties he encounters in the present. However, that does not compel him to reject the present as dull, insipid, rootless and disaffectionate instead, the poet gradually learns to mould his sensibility to accept and embrace such changes or uncertainties of the present and identity himself with the place and its milieu. And, once such identification is complete as in the "Homecoming", the poet acclimatizes his own self into the grand flow of his native tradition.

The poet devotes the next two sections to the memory of his father. He recollects his sense of loneliness in the wake of his father's death. Most painfully does he become aware of his sense of mortality. At the same time, he understands that his present identity is a reflection of his father's, and without this reflected identity there would be no end to his loneliness and despair:

> I am my father now.
> The lines of my hands
> Hold the fine compass of his going:
> I shall follow, and after me,
> My unborn son, through the eye of
> The needle of forgetfulness. (52)

The man, who once had a dream of settling in England as an English poet, comes to realize that his identity springs from his father's. He clings to his past and strengthens his bondage with family that was about to get lost in the illusory euphoria of whoring after the English gods:

> I see myself in you,
> As you bend, daily, our world to yours. (53)

The fluidity of each section of the *Rough Passage* is striking. The 'Exile' section retains the seeds of suffering of 'Trial' and the seeds of hope of 'Homecoming'. The 'Trial' section flows back to 'Exile' in preserving the seeds of loneliness, and moves forward to foreshadow of the possibility of 'Homecoming'. The 'Homecoming' retains the seeds of loneliness of 'Exile' and 'Trial'. This inter-dependence of one section on the other and inflow of one into the other lends unity and continuity to *Rough Passage*.

After his father's death the poet has become lonelier, more acutely conscious of growing old. The burden of his strangeness to himself with the passing of time seems to be lessened by his awareness of a semblance between himself and his father. This is the only redeeming feature in the poet's plight of loneliness:

> Often confront a stranger
>
> In the scratched glass, older
>
> Perhaps, who resembles my father. (54)

Parthasarathy then turns the telescope of his memory towards the mother, with a view to liberating himself from the burden of strangeness about himself and reaffirming his sense of rootedness to a family that had moulded his identity with certain distinctiveness. The poet recollects the memory of 'sniffs at mother's turmeric days' (55) at Nanjangud. He recollects the photograph of his uncle sleeping on his mother's lap. He believes that the strength and vitality of his childhood spring from the 'scalloped folds' of his mother's sari.

The next poem on the river Vaikai reminds one of Ramanujan's poems in Madurai. Ramanujan registers the truth about the river—its strange moods, its strange uses. Rarely does the river flood, but when it does, it brings infinite misery to the people. But Parthasarathy ruefully images forth the frighteningly decadent plight of the river. The river is a symbol of perpetuity of life and civilization, it relates one to one's past. But the poet is unhappy about the miserable degeneration of the river, Vaikai. Boys 'tickle her ribs' with paper boats. Buffaloes have turned into a pond. People clean their cloths on the steps.

And further he writes:

> She is become
>
> A sweer, now. No one has any use for
>
> Vaikai, river, once, of this sweet city. (56)

The scene changes from the river Vaikai at Madurai to rock-cut stone temples at Mamallapuram. The many-clawed sea has the historically significant Mamallapuram on its shore, which is now a hot place visited by 'Humped tourists,/ Kodak's around their necks', the river Vaikai at Madurai and the temples of Mamallapuram are the important milestones of Tamil culture. The poet sees them decayed beyond revival. Yet he is aware that at the centre of a Tamil consciousness lies buried the importance of such places as Madurai or Mamallapuram. The sense of belonging to such a rich and glorious culture is in itself the manifestation of Parthasarathy's home/nation bound vision. Such moorings not only vindicate the poet's quest for roots, but his sense of involvement and identification with his home, society and the nation.

Parthasarathy's poetry posits a shift in the patterning of the imagery—from personal to regional level. It is, however, an indication of the poet's positive attitude, in so far as the poet involves and identifies himself with the varying strands of native cultural, social and familial moorings.

'Homecoming 12' is also an objective study of the pilgrim's career as a poet and as a husband. He comes to realize that his that his past is an unpolished stone. It brings in a horde of memories of his marriage, the futility of his whoring after wrong gods, and the meaninglessness of reviewing books and writing poems. The poet's sense of agony and isolation gets intensified with the objective study of himself. He halts for a while to measure the heights of his achievement, both as a creative writer and as a family man. Using irony, the poet mocks at himself:

> I say to myself, 'The son of a bitch'
> Fattens himself on the flesh of dead poets,
> Lines his pockets with their blood. (60)

He realizes that depending fully on the 'dead poets' for his own creativity is perhaps an act of foolishness.

Parthasarathy further realizes that as a modern poet, he must invent for himself an idiom and a medium. Like Ramanujan, he looks at the past critically, plunges deep into his bygone days to rediscover a usable past for himself and moulds his sensibility to embrace any change or uncertainty to the present.

The next section of 'Homecoming' reiterates the pilgrim's sense of isolation. He lives off friends, burns out his files with the fear that 'they would close in' on him, he plucks grey hairs from his forehead and follows the smoke of his cigarette 'as though it were a private route'. The poet feels that there is something compellingly interesting about the privatization of the self, and this is the way he can choose to articulate his own vision of a home-coming.

'Homecoming 14' once again harps on the significant images, already used in 'Exile' and 'Trial'. The poet's sense of being an exile in his own country is reemphasized but with a subtle difference. At least, the way-farer poet gets the satisfaction and warmth of reaching the threshold of his home, although tied:

> I return home, tried
>
> My face pressed against the window
>
> of expectation. (63)

This open-hearted willingness to remain contended with life as it is, is the beginning of disapproval of his exilic mode of existence, and in certain positive ways, the end of a period of restless existence through 'Exile' and 'Trial'.

Subhas Saha rightly observes this change in the poet, who he sees as a pilgrim in quest of his home, his pilgrimage, as the beginning of an ethical rode of existence.

Saha argues:

> The poet moves from the experiences of frustration and waste to a philosophy of positive acceptance of facts. This development of a positive attitude has an ethical nuance. The effect of this positive progressive attitude on his verbal craftsmanship has been a salubrious one. He has developed a style of his own, a distinctively personal voice. The language has not lost colour under another sky, rather has sucked immense nourishment from the fertilizer of Parthasarathy's typically Indian mind. (Saha 79)

In an alien land and alien culture, the poet gets lost. But, in the course of his journey, he realizes that the self can retain harmony with a place, its milieu and its people, who embody its own roots.

Parthasarathy in an interview with Paniker makes his stance clear and declares his intention to write in Tamil:

> I have started writing in Tamil, and in fact, I'm working on a sequence which I have tentatively called Thiruvarangathi

> and this takes off from where Rough Passage ended; it will be largely a series of exploratory poems about my own Tamil upbringing, childhood and above all, it would attempt a redefinition of myself as a Tamil, what it means to be a Tamil after having gone through all that. (Paniker 21)

Critics and scholar have rightly painted art that Parthasarathy's poetry is image-oriented, and there is the subtle play of irony throughout *Rough Passage*. Sharp, clear, unambiguous images from the bedrock of Parthasarathy's poetry without any proliferating verbiage, the poet harps on the exactness of the experience. If at times the image-pattern bears an intellectual fervour or cerebral twist (Deshpande 14), it is due to the poet's confronting of the intricate experience of life's ordinariness. It is also perhaps due to the poet's awareness of writing in a language that is not native to his tongue. Sivaramkrishna's observation on the use of image as the basic unit of poetic expression in the poetry of Parthasarathy and Ramanujan is noteworthy:

> While in Ramanujan there is emphasis on the immediate context, in Parthasarathy an image has an extended application, and often its connotative richness is available for scrutiny only in the total context of its recurring use. One can say that in one case it's microscopic, in the other, it's prismatic. (Sivaramkrishna 167)

The poet's return to Tamil Nadu or the Tamil tradition, in many ways, registers a positive and affirmative note. At the same time, his intention is clear. He tries to hint at the peculiar ironical situation of the individual. The poet rejects 'English' and comes to initiate a dialogue with Tamil, knowing fully well that it's a tried language. Similarly, in 'Homecoming 2', the poet presents his predicament of helplessness through a propositional statement:

> To live in Tamil Nadu is to be
>
> conscious everyday of importance. (50)

This feeling of importance is further transmitted through the image of the language as an 'unrecognizable carcass, full of fleas of Kodambakkam' (50). The poet intelligently sums up his own helplessness about the situation of language and of the place:

> There is little you can do about it,
>
> Except throw up your hands. (50)

This realization ultimately steers the poet to accept the objective reality without any scintillating sentimentality. This realization too shapes his vision as a poet and a native, which equips him to quietly accept life's unpredictable uncertainties.

Thus the discovery of the self and its relation to the roots the native culture and tradition is the primary motif of *Rough Passage*. Parthasarathy justifies this motif in two ways: first, by structuring the narrative in a three-tier system; second, by bringing English close to the nuances of Tamil language, thereby heralding a new tradition in Indian English.

At last the poet finds himself rooted to his home through his own poetry:

> Life at forty-five,
> Is a breath of fresh air.
> The children are grown up.
> Their eyes hone
> My nights: I soften to the touch.
> The wife keeps house.
> From afar shapes the poems
> Till they become familiar as prayer.
> To be oneself, strike no postures,
> On rare occasions stumble upon
> The blessing of simplicity—
> I couldn't ask for more. (New Letters 84)

Thus the poet's journey comes to a close as it comes full circle. He is, in essence, a home-bound pilgrim.

Ujjall Dutta argues:

> There is a feeling, partly fostered by himself, that Parthasarathy's fulfilment lies in identifying himself with his Tamil past, and that he is moving in that direction. But

> to my mind, his concern with his Tamil past is only one of the much punctuation in the process of self-definition; it is not really home-coming. For there is no marked lifting of the sense of living in parts in the 'Homecoming' group. These poems are as tentative, as exploratory, speaking from the viewpoint of his personal disquietude as those of 'Trial' or 'Exile'. (Dutta 91-92)

The quest-motif ingrained within the journey metaphor comes to a close in the 'Homecoming' section. There is an implicit suggestion of the fulfilment of the poet's quest for his identity. He has been able to come to terms with his roots—Tamil language and Tamil culture. 'Homecoming' is a synthesis between the subjective self and the objective world, between the individual and the tradition.

N'gugi suggests that one is return to one's own language is not easy and feasible. There is inevitability about this inheritance even in the postcolonial situation.

Rough Passage not only registers Parthasarathy's disenchantment with time, place and language but also, in a way, evinces the possible means of overcoming and rising above such disenchantment. The transcendence has been effected partly by the poet's willingness to accept things as they are, and partly by his desire to discover for himself a usable past.

Like all postcolonial poets, Parthasarathy realizes the significance of his own roots—as an individual and as a poet. The poet, therefore, makes a wholehearted attempt to come back to his home where he would get warmth, love and security so that he would no longer feel alienated.

5

Kamala Das

Kamala Das is one of the best known contemporary Indian Poets writing in English. Her name is almost synonymous with Indian English poetry. Her volumes of poetry are best known for honest exploration of the self and female sexuality, urban life, women's role in traditional Indian society, issues relating to postcolonial identity and the personal struggles of marginalized people. She is a highly gifted and skilful writer fully aware of the value of words and their finer shades of meaning, and she has a genius for intimately registering the idiom of her own world. She has created a new Indian English idiom which was unknown to poetic diction. And this new idiom, has given a local habitation and a name to contemporary Indian English poetry. Her works in English has been widely anthologized in India, Australia and the west. Kamala Das has received many prestigious awards which include P.E.N. Phillippines Asian Poetry Prize (1963), Kendra Sahitya Academy Award (1969), Chiman Lal Award for fearless Journalism (1971), The ASIAN World Prize (1985), and the Central Sahitya Akademi Award for her poetry in English (1985). In 1984, she was nominated for the Nobel Prize in Literature.

Kamala Das was born in an aristocratic Hindu Nair Family in Malabar Kerala on March, 1934. She first attended a European School in Calcutta, then an elementary School at Punnayurkulam and a boarding school run by the Roman Catholic nuns. While at the Catholic boarding school, she fell ill and was shifted to Calcutta where private tutors were engaged to teach her fine arts. Her love for poetry began at an early age by the influence of her maternal great-uncle, Narayan Menon, a prominent writer, and her mother, Balamani Amma, a well-known Malayali poet. Her finest poem was published by P.E.N. India when she was fourteen. Kamala Das got married at the age of fifteen to an official in the Reserve Bank of India, Bombay. But her marital life became miserable as her husband was uncaring, who had no time to spare for her as he was a workaholic. Kamala Das, as a newly wedded wife, was expected to discharge her domestic chores and fulfil the needs and comforts of her husband. The anger and despair of the harassment and ill treatment meted out to her vents out in a rare spark of frankness of expression:

> You called my wife,
> I was taught to break saccharine into your tea and
> to offer at the right moment the vitamins. Cowering
> beneath your monstrous ego I ate the magic loaf and
> Become a dwarf. I lost my will and reason, to all your
> Questions I mumbled incoherent replies. The summer
> Begin to fail. (*The Old Playhouse & Other Poems* 1)

Her husband's career took her to Calcutta, New Delhi and Bombay. Her stay in the metropolis not only influenced her poetry it also made her feel the pulse of the whole India. Unlike Parthasarathy or Ramanujan, Kamala Das is firmly rooted in the Indian soil, and her identity is to be found in being rooted. Her poetry registers her response to the landscape of her country, her sense of tradition and culture of the land of her birth.

Kamala Das writes both in English and in Malayalam. She has published eleven books in her mother tongue, and her poetical collection in English are: *Summer in Calcutta* (1965), *The Descendants* (1967), and *The Old Playhouse and Other Poems* (1973) and *Collected Poems* (1984). She has collaborated with Pritish Nandy in *Tonight, This Savage Rite* (1979): a Collection of their love poems. Her autobiography, *My Story*, was serialized in *The Current* weekly of Bombay from January to December, 1974. She has also published a novel in English under the title, *Alphabet of Lust* (1976). Her prose written after *The Descendants* between 1968 and 1976 is almost autobiographical.

Besides her poetical and prose works, she has written extensively for various popular magazines and periodicals, such as *Opinion*, *The Illustrated Weekly of India*, *Poetry East and West*, *Debonair*, *Eve's Weekly*, *Femina*, *Imprint and Weekly Round Table*. She has also contributed short stories in Malayalam for *Mathubhumi* and poems for the Illustrated Weekly. In her Autobiography, she admits:

> I typed nearly a thousand words a week. I wrote about the subjects the editors asked me to write on, fully aware that I was uneducated by the usual standards and that I had no business meddling in grave matters. But I happily meddled to satisfy that particular brand of readers who liked me and liked my honest approach. I was useless as a housewife anyway. I could not pick up a teapot without grasping for breath. But writing was possible. And it certainly brought me happiness. (*My Story*, 218)

Her autobiography evinces that even during her illness; Kamala Das never gave up writing.

Kamala's poetry deals with both the external and the internal worlds. Her internal world embodies inner restlessness, a sense of dirt, anguish and sexual disgust, which her poetry registers with admirable poise and perfection. Her writing explores a sense of identity, intensely personal experiences, including her growth into womanhood, her unsuccessful quest for love in and outside her marriage, her roles of unhappy woman, unhappy wife and mistress to young men, which drive her to a nymphomaniac pining for the lost joys of innocence and childhood in the blissful repose of her Nalapat house in Malabar, her matriarchal rural home. Malabar, the place of her nativity, embodies the physical and emotional values, and the Nalapat house, her ancestral home, is the quintessential soul. Devastated by life's betrayals and scornful love and battered by unhappiness and frustration, Kamala Das often escapes to her past, her childhood joy and innocence she has left behind in her Nalapat house. Her escape to childhood is an escape from the despair and chaotic situation experienced by her female self. It is quest for self, her identity and her Nair background. If the Nalapat house is one of the recurring symbols in Kamala's poetry, it is so because of its inspiring association. It is the poet's heritage house; stands for rootedness and eternity, and its intimates are her blood's inseparable ties. For Kamala Das, Malabar and the Nalapat house, her home, is the most secure place for rest, repose, pleasure and happiness. It is where the dreams wait for her.

Kamala Das's poetry is a truthful record of her life story. The whole gamut of her poetical works deal with love's labour lost, her grandmother and/or the other members of her family, and her ancestral Nalapat house.

Marriage, home making, child rearing, and maintaining the traditional etiquette of the family is some of the dictums that define her as a woman in the prevailing culture of the patriarchal society. A male-dominated society decries a female's ego and fails to look deep into the pathos that woman undergoes for maintaining her responsibilities that is being imposed upon her in the name of tradition and culture. This authoritative phenomenon is conventional in the length and breadth of our nation. Women exist here by sacrificing their dreams and desires. A woman has never been treated more than a sexual object in the eyes of a chauvinistic man. A chauvinistic person perceives the body of the woman as something to control and an object to satisfy his lust. Kamala Das tries to give voice to the deep, concealed emotions of the women because she thinks that probably through literature these agonies and pains can be given the recognition it deserves (Roy 131). She derives her inspiration to write from her own personal life, her own personal experiences. In such poems, Kamala's feminine sensibility finds its true and fullest expression, where the poet's sincerity of feeling and emotions, the agony, anguish and the ecstasy go together. As a wife, Kamala was devoted to her husband with the hope that marriage had sanctioned a blissful conjugal life. She always believed that the real value of married life lies in the depth of union and density of togetherness. Her poems "A Relationship" and "In Love" show how the poet craved for the company of her husband and for a love beyond the pleasure. But there were lines when she felt she was scorned and betrayed. Her poem "I Shall Some Day" records her anguish when she cries that love words have flung away from her man and his lust is tried. Frustration and lovelessness haunt her. She struggles for love and security to disperse her loneliness and frustration. While seeking freedom from displeased conjugality, the poet is often driven to enter others' lives, but at the same time she is aware that entering others' lives can neither fulfil her lust nor can it make a permanent home for her. In her all poems there is an intense and persistent craving to live among relationship. In her love poems, Kamala Das posits herself as a poet of love from a woman's point of view, and she has inherited her bold and straightforward treatment of love and sex from her Nair background.

Kamala Das does not like to subjugate herself to the male-dominated Indian society. She raises her voice against the tradition attitude of men towards women in her poem, "The Stone Age":

> You turn me into a bird of stone, a granite
> Dove, you build round me a shabby drawing room
> And stoke my pitted face absent-mindedly while
> you read. With loud talk you bruise my pre-morning sleep
> You stick a finger into my dreaming eye. (49)

In 'Of Calcutta' she exposes her inner pangs that stem from the customs and rituals and marriage:

> I was sent away, to protect a family's
> Abstractions, sent to another city to be
> A relative's wife, a housefrau for his home, and
> A mother for his sons, yet another nodding
> Doll for his parlour, a walkie talkie one to
> Warm his bed at night. (*Collected Poems* 59)

She admits that in her husband's home she is reduced to a 'trained circus dog' (*Collected Poems* 59). She craves for freedom, as she feels that in love and marriage, the centre is not the blind worship of husband but the consummation of love. She longs for tenderness that she lost years back in her childhood. Recollection of the past emancipates her from the fruitless present, her present anguish and agonies. Her escape to childhood obviously gives a new rearing to her present. The recollection serves as a mode of redemption as it is an escape from the despair and chaotic situations experienced by her female self.

In her lonesome moments she recollects her grandmother—the source of tenderness and unselfish love. One of the central characters in Kamala Das's work is her grandmother who is inseparably linked with her memory of the parental home. She felt at home, and got her diseases cured. She describes her grandmother's house as a paradise on earth. In "My Grandmother's House" (*Summer in Calcutta*), she celebrates the Nalapat house as the seat of her great comfort, abounding in love and life.

> There is a house now four away where once.
> I received love.... That woman died,
> The house withdrew into silence, snakes
> Among books I was then too moved young
> To read, and my blood turned cold like the moon
> How often I think of going
> There....

Kamala's recollection of the images of the old house besides the heating sea can be traced back to her childhood associations with it. While comparing A.K. Ramanujan's "Small Scale Reflections on Great House" with "My Grandmother's House", it can be seen that Ramanujan's attitude is chronic, whereas Kamala Das's attitude remains reverential and affectionate.

Living in the disaffectionate present, she misses her grandmother, whose memory serves as a window through which she relates herself to the lost home, and the lost innocence of her childhood. She recollects those nights when her grandmother would be waiting for her with a dim lantern burning in her room of the four-hundred year old family home:

> We shall talk, she said darling,
> We shall talk all night and,
> In the evening, she kept a lighted

lantern on the window-sill, and sat up
waiting for me. (*The Old Playhouse* 7)

The granny symbolizes not only love and tenderness but her home to which she always intends to return. Once, the granny narrated the deplorable condition of the old family house. She wished that her grandchildren would repair the ancient building to preserve the relics of ancient blood. The poet could do nothing to preserve the ancestral home. She expresses her utter helplessness when the granny dies:

When they burnt my great grandmother
Over logs of the mango tree
I looked once at the house
And then again and again
For I saw the windows close
Like the closing of the eyes
I thought I heard the pillars groan
And the dark rooms heave a sigh. (18)

In yet another poem, "My Grandmother's House", Das's woes seem to multiply as she is cut off from the granny for ever:

There is a house now far away where once I received
Love.... That woman dies, the house withdrew into
Silence, snakes moved. Among books I was then too
Young to read, and my blood turned cold like the
Moon. How often I think of going. There, to peer
through blind eyes of windows or just listen to the
frozen air. Or in wild despair, pick an armful of
Darkness to bring it here to lie
behind my bedroom like a brooding Dog. (32)

The mounting years of ageing hangs heavy on the poet. But the grandmother remains the ultimate source of solace to her. She is haunted by the absence of the grandmother and hence the unassuaged world:

Eighteen years have passed since my grandmother's death:
I wonder why the ache still persists. Was
She buried, bones and all, in the loose red
Soil of my heart? All through the sun singing
Day, all through the moon wailing night, I think
Of her, of the warmth that she took away,
Wrapped in funerary white, a fire that
Stayed lit while her blood cooled and there was no
More of it for me, for, no longer was
There someone to pour an arm around my
Shoulders without a purpose. (*Collected Poems* 97)

"My Grandmother's House" is a fond recollection of grandma's love, who is now dead. It is a search for relationship and the poet is well aware that intimacy of relationship binds the family and it is relationship alone that concretizes the home/nation. When her grandmother passed away, Kamala Das was deprived of love and affection, because other "blood-ties" do not satisfy ('Composition' 5). Kamala Das's close intimacy with her grandmother whom she shared blissful moments and togetherness, is related to her inseparable bond with the Nalapat house. Her heart feels the pinch when she revisits her past:

The years have
Spend along, stopping briefly
At beloved halts. (*Summer in Calcutta* 45)

The vision of Nalapat house and Malabar and all the memories associated with her past enlivens in her and excites her. It makes her nostalgic and reminiscent in "A Hot Noon in Malabar". Along with the loss of her granny, Das mourns the loss of her father:

We are tongue-tied, humbled and quiet
Although within we wept for you
And more for ourselves, now without a guardian.
Who would send us money to bail us out of jail.

Who would come when we land as junk at the city hospitals. (*Collected Poems* 39)

In yet another poem "Forest Fire", Das wants to create a mother-oriented society by remembering her mother and placing herself in a mother's role as well. In fact, she makes an effort to play different roles, such as mother, wife and daughter. Such pining for her role for her family offers a strong vision of home/family and the familial ties and a desire to recapture/rebuild it.

Kamala Das's Poetry shows a strong mark of subjectivism. She is a victim of circumstances and displeased conjugality. Her quest for true love lands her up in disasters. Her poetry is autobiographical as it depicts her personal experiences in matters of love and sex. In the "Descendants" her subjective feeling are predominant:

But,
I must pose,
I must pretend,
I must act the role
Of happy woman,
Happy wife. ('The Suicide' 2)

In "Composition," she says:

What I am able to give
Is only what your wife is qualified
to give.
We are all alike,
We women,
In our wrappings of hairless skin.

Failure to find satisfaction with her man and she was driven into other's arms:

I enter other's
Lives, and
Make of every trap of lust
A temporary home. (21)

These lines show her moral degradation and, at the same time her emotional urges of unfulfilled love. She draws the readers' attention to herself, again and again, and that's why she writes 'I' and 'my' and 'mine' which shows her strong subjectivism.

Her hallow marital relationship comes under fire in the poem "Captive":

> My love is an empty gift, a gilded
> Empty container, good for show nothing else.
> (*The Descendants* 17)

"Composition" brings to the fore the rottenness of her body and the uselessness of her love-pranks. She writes:

> To be frank,
> I have failed.
> I feel my age and my
> Uselessness. (*The Descendants* 34)

In 'A Relationship' she writes about the dire necessity of the man:

> Yes,
> It was my desire that made him male
> And beautiful, so that when at last we
> Met, to believe that one I knew not his
> Form, his quiet touch, or the bind kindness
> Of his lips was hard indeed. (*Summer in Calcutta* 18)

In "Loud Posters", she writes:

> I've stretched my two dimensional
> Nudity on sheets of weeklies, monthlies,
> Quarterlies.... (*Summer in Calcutta* 23)

In 'The Looking Glass' she portrays the beauty and charm of a woman and secret of a true love-making:

> Getting a man to love you is easy
> Only he honest about your wants as
> Woman. Stand nude before the glass with him

So that he sees himself the stronger one.
And believe it so, and you so much more
Softer, younger, lovelier.... Admit your
Admiration. Notice the perfection
Of his limbs, his eyes reddening under
Shower, the shy walk across the bathroom floor,
Dropping towels, and the jerky way he
Urinates. All the fond details that make
Him male and your only man.

Kamala Das express her impression about the behaviour and attitude towards her husband and, at the same time, she criticises her husband who is a large man of lust and cruelty, having no respect for her feelings and emotion. In the 'Convicts' she says:

That was the only kind of love,
This hacking at each other's parts
Like convicts hacking, breaking clods
At noon. We were earth under hot sun.
(*The Descendants* 26)

Kamala uses bitter imagery to express the energy and the violence in the sexual intercourse in the summer season. There is a sense of guilt over such an involvement conveyed by the metaphor 'convicts'. But her boldness and frankness of expression, and the use of new, unconventional words are undoubtedly rare in Indian English diction.

Kamala Das never hates the physical body; rather she conveys her pleasure-experience in the company of her lover. In "winter", she frankly admits:

And, I loved his body without shame,
On winter evenings as cold winds
Chuckled against the white window panes
(*Summer in Calcutta* 17)

In "The Music Party" she writes about her desire for looking at her man unashamedly before things go wrong for her:

I wish my
Eyes were similarly
Brave and had looked at you
At least once before the
Singing stopped and you left
Quickly, without goodbye.... (*Summer in Calcutta* 34)

The poet seems to say that sex and sensuality are a part of life, and if one has to accept art for art's sake one has to affirm sensuality.

The poet makes ample use of images and symbols for 'ornamentation' of her writing and for arousing 'aesthetic pleasure' in the reader. Her images and symbols reveal her artistic skill and craftsmanship. She celebrates the human body as a gift of God. To her the male body symbolizes corruption and exploitation, the female body is a house of beauty and chastity. Prof. K.R.S. Iyengar has rightly recognised Kamala's aggressive individualistic talent which enables her to express feminine sensibility to articulate the hurts it has received in an insensitive largely man made world:

In 'The Freaks' (*Summer in Calcutta*) the poetess has drawn an ugly picture of the love lorn man, 'a sun—stained cheek', 'a dark cavern' in mouth, and 'uneven teeth'. She is not at all happy in his company and when she complains:

You dribbled spittle into my mouth, you poured
Yourself into every nook and cranny, you embalmed
My pour lust with your bitter sweet juices.
(*The Old Playhouse and Other Poems* 1)

The image in these lines evokes the saturation in sex-act and at the same time highlights her sense of bitterness in his contact. In "The Stone Age" she express her dislike of the man. As she writes:

Ask me, everybody, ask me,
What he sees in me, ask me why he is called a
A libertine, ask me the flavour of his

Mouth, ask me why his hand sways like a hooded snake
Before it clasps my pubis. Ask me why like
A great tree, felled, he slumps against my breasts,
And sleeps (*The Old Playhouse and Other Poems* 51)

She does not relish 'the flavour of his mouth' and the way he 'claps her pubes' and the image of a 'hooded snake' shows the craftsmanship use of the poet. It speaks about a mood of frenzied passion. Kamala Das was married to an insensitive and unsympathetic man who devoted all his time to the official files and had no leisure to spare for his wife. No doubt, he tried his best to earn money for the family, but that was not enough to satisfy her. She feels like a helpless bird put in a cage. Writing on her husband, she says:

My husband was immerged in his office-work,
And after work there was the dinner, followed
by sex. Where was there any time left for him
To want to see the sea or the dark buffaloes
Of the slopes? (*Debonair* III 1975: 41)

A.N. Dewivedi has rightly observed:

> Kamala Das is a delightful poet of love and sex, unravelling the mysteries of the finer sex in this matter. The 'Openness' and the 'honesty' that we find in her is rarely witnessed in other Indo-English women poets, with the possible exception of Gauri Deshpande in a lesser degree. In fact, many others contemporary Indian poets have sung songs in honour of love—such poets as Shiv K. Kumar, Pritish Nandy, Nissim Ezekiel, Parthasarathy, Jayanta Mahapatra, and A.K. Ramanujan—but in her emotional sweep and lyrical rapture Kamala Das surpasses them all. Love is citadel where her personal cares and anxieties, her own dilemmas and predicaments, are safely anchored. (Dwivedi 39)

Kamala Das is a conscientious artist. She is aware of the value of words and their meaning. The selection and choice of words, phrases and expressions are meticulous and precise. In her poem, "Words", she says:

But I tell myself, words
Are a nuisance, beware of them they
Can be so many things..... (*Summer in Calcutta* 11)

In the poem "Convicts", she pinpoints the futility of 'Words':

There were no more
Words left, all words lay imprisoned
In the aging arms of might. (*The Descendants* 26)

In her well-known poem, "An Introduction", Kamala speaks out her mind with regard to the question of using 'the English language'. Kamala Das exercises a special care in her use of idioms and combination of those words into phrase, clauses and sentences. She shows a rare understanding of the meanings, the appropriateness, and the subtleties of words. She is in the confessional mode; her poetry is lyrical, conversational in tone and colloquial in speech. The words come to her effortlessly, and become one with her emotions. This is evident in "My Grandmother's House", "A Hot Noon in Malabar", "An Introduction". Her diction is highly commendable because of the appropriateness of the words used and the felicitous manner in which she has arranged those words in poems. A felicity in the use of words and in phrase-making thus constitutes one of the outstanding features of her poetry. Simplicity, ease and grace characterize her style. But when she expresses her emotions, her language assumes the felicity of expression. Lend Hess has rightly observed the 'original poetic voice' in Mrs Das:

> ...a genuine poetic talent is at work here. It lives in every page, is woven even through the most distressingly flawed poems. And in a few superb pieces it stands forth unchallenged and unmistakable. (Kohli 38)

Her poetry makes the best use of figures of speech. Her alienation breathes fire and fury at places. The use of simile is befitting to her emotions. In "Drama" she likens a 'a red, red lamp' to 'an angry Sun' while the 'Stone Age' compares the sway of 'his hand' to a 'hooded snake'. In 'Forest Fire' her application of simile is remarkable:

Of late I began to fell a hunger
To take in with greed, like a forest fire
Consumes, and, with each killing gains a wilder
Brighter charm all that comes my way.
(*The Old Playhouse* 39)

It is opt to say that her poetry is based largely on the physical aspects of a female, whereas feminine sensibility, in real term implies stress on emotional bond. In other poem like "Annettle", "Convicts", "Gino", "Nani", Kamala uses beautiful similes to serve her purpose. Her use of metaphor is perfect in a noticeable manner. In "Substitute" she writes:

After that love became a Swivel-door,
when one went out, another came in.
Then I lost count, for always in my arm
Was a substitute for substitute? (*The Descendants* 7)

Her deft use of the metaphor of love that is made a 'swivel-door' refers to the frequent change of lovers indicated by the opening and closing of the door. The line shows an urge for love where many persons entered her life, but she doesn't make any efforts to hide it.

As an Indian poet firmly rooted in the native soil, culture and tradition, Kamala Das uses the Indian myths and symbols perfectly. The myth of 'Radha Krishna' assumes the shape of a recurrent symbol in her poetry. She is pessimistic in her outlook on life and applies this myth as a symbol for her salvation. Her unflinching devotion to Lord Krishna lead her to identify herself with the Lord. In my story, she writes:

There was an imaginary life running parallel to
Our real life. I filled his (her son's) childhood
With magic and wonder. Always he smiled
With the sheer happiness of being alive.
He sat on my knee looking like the infant
Krishnan. (195)

These lines show her devotion and faith to Lord Krishna. She imagines herself as Radha seeking the divine love incarnate as Krishnan. In *Summer in Calcutta*, 'Radha Krishna', she displays her aversion for physical love which her husband stands for. In another poem, "Radha", she identifies with the Lord, and writes:

And virgin crying
Everything in me
Is melting, even the hardness at the core
O Krishna, I am melting, melting, melting
Nothing remains
You.... (*The Descendants* 9)

These lines show how the poet aspires for eternal love, and for this she would like to melt like a burning candle only for the true love of Krishna. In another poem "Ghanashyama", the poet highlights her deep love for Krishna as she writes:

Ghanashyama,
You have like a koel built your
Nest in the arbour of my heart.
My life, until now a sleeping jungle
Is at last astir with music.

Her devotion to Lord Krishna made her happy and contented. Thus the mythical symbol of Radha and Krishna has come to her rescue and given her peace and solace from a life of dejection and suffering. The use of Indian myths helps create an identity for the poet. Like all postcolonial poets, Kamala Das also makes use of national myths to create an identity of her own by way of resisting and subverting the colonizer.

Kamala Das's poetry at times has repetition and monotony in the body of her poetical works. However, she has never transgressed her self-imposed limitations for success in poetical endeavours. Her choice of English as her creative medium does not distort her identity, but reaffirms her distinctiveness and rootedness as an Indian. She clarifies her stand in 'Introduction':

I'm an Indian, very brown, born in Malabar,
I speak three language, write in two, dream in one....
The language I speak becomes mine, its distortions,
Its queerness all mine, mine alone.
It is half English half Indian,
funny perhaps, but it is honest it is ads human as I human,
don't you see it?
(*The Old Playhouse and Other Poems* 26)

And further she adds:

It voices my joys, my longings, my
Hopes, and it is useful to me as a cawing
Is to cow or roaring to the lions, it is hymn speech,
The speech of the mind that is here and not there,
A mind that sees and hears and is aware.
Not the deaf, blind speech of trees in storm or of
Monsoon clouds or of rain or the incoherent
mutterings of the blazing funeral pyre.
(*Summer in Calcutta* 59)

This is a powerful plea for her use of the English language, whether she 'dreams' in it or in Malayalam. In an interview to P. Lal, she says, "English being the most familiar, we use it. That is all" (April, 1969). This is an open-hearted confession by the poet.

Post-independence Indian English poetry called for a new use of the language and the use of every speech rhythm, creation of an Indian English idiom in order to give an independent identity to it and make it different from other world literatures written in English. Kamala Das has greatly succeeded in creating a new Indian English idiom. Emotions dominate her poetry. Her writings are lucid, honest, accurate and sincere. Her attitude is defiant. She expresses her feminine sensibility with courage, conviction and honesty. She uses her words in English in a typical Indian way with native accent and collocation that befit her emotion and obey her call.

Parthasarathy in *Rough Passage* said that language is a tree loses colour under another sky. But the irony is Parthasarathy himself continues to write poetry in English. Kamala Das has clarified her stand in her poem "An Introduction", where she declares that the language she speaks and writes is her own. Its distortions and queerness too become alone. It may appear funny that the language she uses in her poetry is half English and half Indian, but her language is honest and human, devoid of any hyperbole or hypocrisy. In other words, Kamala Das uses English as an Indian speaks, writes and understands.

Thus Kamala Das is a typical Indian voice in the post-independence Indian English poetry, who seeks to obtain an identity that is lovable and linked to the realities of live. Her poetry reflects her inner compulsion and passion to remain tied to her roots—the Nalapat house, her home, and Malabar. That is why, during her illness from myocarditis followed by a heart attack; she longs to go back to Malabar. Home guarantees love, tenderness and grace; it ensures liberty and security. Such realization at the core of her poetry forms the poet's home/ nation bound vision.

6

Jayanta Mahapatra

Jayanta Mahapatra is the first Oriya poet to carve a niche for himself in Indian English Literature. Like Nissim Ezekiel and A.K. Ramanujan, he is widely read and discussed both at home and abroad irrespective of obscurity, complexity and allusiveness in his poetry. He is a prolific poet, and has never looked back since he published his first book of verse, *Close the Sky Ten by Ten* (1971), followed by *Svaymvara and Other Poems* (1971), *The False Start* (1980), *Waiting* (1979), *Life Signs* (1983) *Dispossessed Nests* (1986), *Burden of Waves and Fruit* (1986), *Temple* (1989), *Shadow Space* (1997), *Bare Face* (2000), *Random Descent* (2005). His poetry shows a continuous development both in theme and technique. He has received many awards including Jacob Glastein Memorial Award (1975), Australia's Cultural Award (1978), Japan Foundation Visitor's Award (1980), Indian Academy of Arts (1981), Indo-Soviet Exchange Writer in the U.S.S.R. (1985), Resident Poet of the Rockfeller Cultural Foundation Award (1986). He was awarded an honorary doctorate degree from Ravenshaw University, Cuttack in 2009 and the Padma Shree Award for his outstanding contribution to the field of Indian English Poetry.

This chapter makes an attempt to study the poetry of Jayanta Mahapatra with a view to identifying the nature and kind of self that remains embedded within. It further makes an attempt to unravel the nature of the self as revealed through the poems. Mahapatra's poetry offers a postcolonial gesture which helps him not only to highlight those areas which were marginalized but also illustrates how they relate themselves to home or family, community and culture as well as the nation as a whole to forge for himself a national identity as a creative writer.

R. Parthasarathy rightly points out that 'Orissa is the hub of Jayanta Mahapatra's iconoclastic perambulations'. M.K. Naik emphasizes on the same strength of Mahapatra's poetry as he says: 'Mahapatra's poetry is redolent of the Orissan scene and the Jagannath temple at Puri figures quite often in it.'

Orissa, popularly known as the land of Lord Jagannath, remains at the core of Mahapatra's creativity. His later poetry is the record of an initiation of a dialogue with his tradition. In a good number of poems Mahapatra tries to evoke an atmosphere of the lost glory, the lost ecstasy of Orissan culture. Mahapatra has rightly stated his view while receiving the National Akademy of Letters award in the following words:

> To Orissa, to this land in which my roots lie and lies my past and in which my beginning and my end, where the wind knees over the grief of the River Daya and where the waves of Bay of Bengal fail to real out today to the twilight soul of Konarka, I acknowledge my debt and my relationship.

Mahapatra's poetic exploration of the places to which he belongs turns out to be a search for the self. A sense of belonging to the place of his birth and the landscape of his state relates him to his poetic craft. He is firmly rooted in the Orissan soil. Puri, Konark, Cuttack and Bhubaneswar form a quadrangle in the landscape of Mahapatra's poetry. Legends, myths, culture and history, associated with these places become the nerve centre of his writings. He wrote a number of poems on Puri, the seat of Lord Jagannath, the presiding deity of Orissan people, and one of the four great sacred places of pilgrimage for the Hindus.

Jayanta Mahapatra's obsession with his native land Orissa, its culture, people and history form the root and rocked of his poetry. Orissa, the land of his birth, the land of art and literature, rich culture and heritage, assumes a metaphoric dimension of home in Mahapatra's poetry through social, historical and cultural implications. The land is central to his poetic consciousness. It is this land in which his roots lie and so does his past. Cuttack, Jayanta Mahapatra's hometown and his birthplace, is not only depicted as a town of joyous festivities but also as famous for its mythical, historical and cultural background ("Waiting"). "The Mahanadi", the majestic river that flows by Cuttack shapes and moulds the destiny of the people of his hometown.

'The Temple Road, Puri' unveils the mystery of human life. The metaphor of life used in the poem shows the possibility of redemption of human folly. The sacrosanct authority, with which the Puri temple stands, cleanses and purifies the devotees crowding its gate:

> Later,
> as the shrines of light
> slowly close their eyes,
> something reaching into them
> from that place they learn to bear
> the lame lamp post
> to the huge temple door,
> the sacred beads in their hands gaping
> at the human ground.

The devotion to the deity transforms the devotees as if they seem to hear the message of the Lord. A sense of universal brotherhood is celebrated by Mahapatra in this poem.

In 'Learning to flow free in the chariot festival at Puri', the poet shows his emotional involvement with the car festival at Puri. At the Car festival, millions pull the divine chariots and watch Lord Jagannath moving through the sea of devotees. Unidentifiable in the vast crowd, the poet watches the divine sojourn of his Lord that illuminates his spirit, and he presents this spiritual illumination within through the metaphor of a corn:

> The giant chariot jostles like a toy
> In a million hands, numbed figures litter the way
> Before the black abyss of its unheard cry,

And in the frail red veins of retinas
Spiders of light finger like cores of blessings.
Watching, my body soon splits open like a cob of corn.
(*Waiting* 32)

Mahapatra's poems on Puri Lord Jagannath uphold the innocence and unflinching faith of the Oriya people in their heritage, culture and tradition 'Konarka' is yet another poem that successfully articulates Mahapatra's obsession with the myths and legends of the place of his birth. The Konark temple is a parallel to life, a manifestation of the temporal dimension of life. The poet breaths life into the temple to seek its timeless dimension lying embodied in the artistic vision it portrays. A legend says that the 12-year old boy Dharma, son of Bisu Maharana, the chief of the masons, put the crowning slab of the Sun Temple. He committed suicide to save the prestige of the twelve hundred masons who were engaged in building the temple.

By delving deep in tradition, myth and legends of his native land, and reliving the a poets, Mahapatra authenticates his identity, legitimizes his voice as typically Oriya/Indian by constructing the images of home and/or the nation. Even when the poet crawls into the autumn of his live, he...forgets his own sense of loss in the process of ageing, when he compares it with the loss grafted in the veins of Oriya tradition:

I must carry the stone I found
In the late afternoon light
Let me not think of myself only,
And my pain which possesses
These last breaths of my life. (*Waiting* 22)

Mahapatra explores through the language of the stones the possibility of coming closer to the language of the myths and the pristine glory of his people. He initiates a dialogue with his racial past through the myths:

Once again one must sit back and bury the face
In this earth of the forbidding myth,
the phallus of the enormous stone. (*Relationship* 9)

It is evident that Mahapatra, in the process of exploring his roots, falls back on the racial past and holds them dearly, so much so that the burden of the self gets deciphered by the redeeming phantasmagoria of the place.

In the poem "Somewhere, My Man" the poet celebrates the process of absorption of man into the place:

> A man does not mean anything
>
> But the place.
>
> sitting on the river bank throwing pebbles
>
> into the muddy current,
>
> a man becomes the place.
>
> Even that simple enough thing. ("A Rain of Rites" 42)

For the post-independence Indian writers writing in English, the place of their nativity holds the key to legitimize their roots and authenticate their voices. They are aware that in their homeland lie embedded their rich culture and tradition, their heritage and post glory, and, above all, the treasured myths and legends. By thoroughly absorbing in and assimilating with the land of their birth, they not only revive the past and speak the pastiness of the past, but at the same time they make the past assert and authenticate their voice in the present, thereby makes an effort to redeem their sense of alienation from home.

Mahapatra's poetry acknowledges his allegiance to the place of his birth. This is perhaps one of the many ways by which the poet tries to redeem his own sense of isolation. Falling back on the past, both familial and cultural, revitalizing the spirits of innocence embedded in the rituals and myths, Mahapatra not only celebrates his sense of belongingness the place but also advocates his willingness to live by them.

The poet shows his concern about the infinite problems of hunger, poverty and dehumanization in his own land. Mahapatra's sense of belongingness and his rootedness to his homeland is vivid in his deep concern for the ebbing values of the once-glorious culture of the land of his birth. However, he feels a sense of gloom, a sense of defeat, a sense of getting older and colder with the passage of time. The sense growing old and graying makes him painfully lonelier than ever.

The poet escapes from the microcosmic self and indulges in the macrocosmic self of his own culture so as to overcome his own sense of loneliness, relatedness, ageing, disease and death. He, therefore, goes on celebrating the secret dimensions of his own ritualistic culture and history in the whole gamut of this poetry. This is perhaps the best possible way in which one cannot only determine the nature of his own self but also can purge the self or its uncertainties. In 'Dhauligiri' (a rock near Bhubaneswar, famous for its inscriptions and the idol of Budha), the poet traces the significance of the Kalinga war, fought between Ashoka and the people of Kalinga, where the former had to relinquish warfare after a bloody victory, and accept Buddhism:

> Afterwards
> when the wars of Kalinga were over,
> the fallow fields of Dhauli
> hid the red-smeared voiceless bodies.
> The place of his pain peer lamentably
> From among the pains of dead.

Mahapatra recalls how emperor Ashoka had once massacred thousands of brave Oriya soldiers on the banks of the River Daya, and the latter being a silent spectator of that dreadful Kalinga war of 261 B.C. for which its water had turned red with the blood of the brave fighters.

Mahapatra's poetry makes an effort to glorify and enhance the history of Orissa. In "Orissa", the poet shows his social, cultural and religious passion along with a nostalgic harping back on the glorious era of Orissa's past. The poem recalls the maritime navigators who once soiled across the seas to trade in far off lands. Similarly, the poem "Konark" vividly delineates the ancient art and architecture of the Black Pagoda and the poet's hope of bridging the chasm that separates him from his origin and his ancestry.

Mahapatra's accessibility to the Hindu myths and rituals, his meditative awareness of the architectonic perfection and excellence of temples, his study of the Oriya psyche, and his sympathy for the destiny-ridden faith of Orissan landscape constitute the unsoiled theme of his poetry. Mahapatra's is a poetry of mystery, a poetry of politeness and hurt that get redeemed through the innocence posited in those omniscient round shaped eyes of the lord. Mahapatra believes that human folly and guilt is redeemable through a living and loving faith in the loving and living Lord Jagannath. Use of myths in his poetry not only sharpens his imagination but strengthens his bondage with the past of his place. Myths are deposits of a culture and they acquaint us with the psychic make up of the people, who use them for the sake of faith and belief.

The poems on Orissa involving its historical and cultural past constitute a shield that defends him against the process which isolate him and create an uneasy fear of death. Relapsing into his private past and the past of his own homeland, the poet deliberates upon escaping from the burdens of the present. But this escapist phantasy should not be taken seriously because it helps him establish a living rapport with the past, and make the present meaningful. Realization of the inevitability of death makes him discover for himself a place which would remain unaffected by the forces of death. Mahapatra honestly believes that a culture never dies, and a place nerve withers away; both allow change and both incorporate movement through changes. It is precisely because of this realization that Mahapatra escapes from his own microcosmic self and involves himself in the macrocosmic and objective world without.

There is a positive change and a distinctive movement towards growth and maturity in the poetic vision which tries to minimize the tension emerging form the isolationist tendency of the self. In his later poetry, Mahapatra has been concerned with the problem of isolation as a poet writing in English which is not his mother tongue. Mahapatra's schooling in English medium and his training as a physicist have contributed to the kind of objectivity he is seeking in his poems. At the same time, it is interesting to observe that his tongue never changes in English.

In a conversation with Norman Simms Mahapatra admits:

> I started writing and using English rather late in life, and all these years have been spent reading books in the English language, nothing else, mostly fiction. I started writing late, my first poem appearing only at forty, and I believe after I had developed a considerable feeling for the language. I do not find myself being inadequate or self-conscious in the use of English, although I might not be using a totally correct language. The only snag which is always not the medium of communication; other languages like Oriya and Hindi being used simultaneously, or a mixture of English and Oriya. That would make the usage different from the English being used by Englishmen or Americans or Australians, but feeling or emotion in poetic terms. So the question of not being able to communicate myself fully to an audience, either Indian or foreign, does not mean much to me. (*The Poetry of Jayanta Mahapatra* 292)

Mahapatra uses English with sophistication and ease and he happens to be the first poet to receive the Central Sahitya Akademi Award for his book *Relationship*. It is true that the creative process requires isolation, and a meditative mood. In this meditative mood, the poet realizes the significance of poetry as the chronicler of the human experiences. In almost all in his poetry the poet tries to define poetry and the kind of intensity poetry creates.

Mahapatra began his creative career writing love poems. His early poetry tried to capture the multiple facets of love, so as to relate it to the meaningful configuration of life. It is only in his early poetry that one discovers an increasing awareness of the fleeting nature of time and the gift of the past as a priceless possession. In a candid confession Mahapatra admitted:

> Yes, I ruefully admit, my first poems were born of love, of loves' selfishness, and of a huge self pity, like the poems of may I admire. ("The Poet's Blues" 10)

Even if, Mahapatra is 'rueful' about his beginning as a romantic poet, it is believed that through his love poetry he could learn how to establish a rapport with the past, the tradition and culture in his later poetry. The interesting part of his earlier poetry is the willing-adherence to the creation of a kind of tension that gives Mahapatra's poetry a rare sophistication. As one moves from the early verse to the later poetry of Mahapatra, one observes a change in the treatment of themes, a shift in the style that is quite unassuming and devoid of any auras of experimentation. Attempt if Mahapatra has matured as a poet achieving a rare perfection in terms of handling themes and style, what remains striking and evident is the nature of the poet's self. The self is isolated partly because of the poetic stance he retains with regard to his self and the world without. It is a truism that isolation is necessary for perpetuating creativity. The reasons of the poet's isolation are stemming more particularly from his relationship with an involvement in the affairs of the family. In a good number of poems, Mahapatra celebrates his family and at places tries to relate himself to the visible and invisible dimensions of home, family and its members, living or dead, with a view to defining precisely his quest for root and his own identity.

Family or home, therefore, assumes a starting proportion in Mahapatra's poetry. It has both the positive and negative side-family as long as it stretchers the poet's identity and saves him from the loss of face, and as long as it becomes a veritable link between past, present and future, Mahapatra does not shrink from celebrating family as a gifted metaphor. In fact, he is conscious of the changes, the losses that creep into the family slowly. There is a pervading sense of gloom and melancholy sparing from his early to later poetry. The enormity of loss which Mahapatra experiences and explicates in his poetry stems partly from the past and partly from the present. It stems from the past because, it happened or existed once, and it cannot be achieved except in memory. It terms of a system of values which once governed our existence. Besides, the poet encounters loneliness, betrayal, hunger, poverty, violence, disease and death everywhere. In trying to seek redemption from the disease-ridden present, when the poet falls back on the past, he is wounded too. Both in the past and in the present, man's suffering is inevitable. The poet feels hurt when he sees the lack of sympathy and respect for human beings:

He writes:

> Always, someone somewhere
> is denying someone else his dignity.
> Someone's porcelain face is always laughing.
> Someone makes the dead walk in the night.
> (*Random Descent* 42)

Loss of dignity is loss of human values and identity. This dichotomy haunts the poet. He criticizes the brute in a modern man whose sole aim is to strike the iron when it is hot. In 'Hunger', the poet gives a realistic picture which could happen to the poverty-stricken fisherman of Gopalpur on sea. The old fisherman offers his 15-year-old daughter to the tourists to enjoy for the sake of a little money. The girl is a commodity for the father to earn livelihood for the survival of his family. As he writes:

> The fisherman said, she's just turned fifteen....
> Feel her. I'll be back soon; your bus leaves at nine.
> ("A Rain of Rites" 44)

Hunger has become a metaphor for sexual desire, which shows Mahapatra's sensitive experience. It is an impressive authentic voice which exhibits the poet's skill as a mature poet writing in English.

"Mahapatra finds poetry raising out of the remnants, ashes, graveyards, the hunger of children, the quiet anguish of women, and the suffering and frustration of the poor and oppressed of the land and in fact, the whole country" (Kallury 60). The sense of alienation that he experienced in his father's house gives way to a rootedness in the land and history.

Vilas Sarang rightly comments:

> The poetry of Mahapatra is extremely local and his tone of quiet acceptance, with a latent awareness of centuries of suffering indicates a very Indian sensibility. He effortlessly translates a profoundly Indian spirit into English. (Sarang 31-32)

In 'Grand Father' Mahapatra holds his grandfather responsible for the gloom in the family because of his absence. His grandfather embraces Christianity during the terrible famine that struck Orissa in 1966. The rediscovery of the memories of his grandfather through the yellow diary becomes both an expression of joy and sorrow—joy because the poet could hold it dearly; sorrow because the grandfather is absent forever:

> The yellowed diary's notes whisper in vernacular.
>
> They sound the forgotten posture,
>
> The cramped cry that forces me to hear that voice.
>
> Now I stumble in you black-paged wake. (*Life Signs* 20)

In the absence of the grandfather the poet regrets that he should have known the patriarch more intimately and closely even in his absence. The grandfather blesses the poet and his family, and the poet is fortunate enough to recognize the glories of inheritance:

> A conscience of years is between us. He is young. The whirls of glory are breaking down for him before me. Does he think of the past, as a loss we have lived our own? Out of silence we look back now at what we do not know. There is a dawn waiting besides as, whose signs are a hundred odd years away from you, Grandfather. (*Life Signs* 20)

In 'The way of the river' the poet tries to collect the pebbles of his identity following the slow flow of the river across the sal and deodar jungles of the ancestral past. While moving along the banks, he realizes the existence would have gathered no meaning without the blessing of his father and forefathers:

> Tonight I know that the life I have lived
>
> is my life softened in my father's life....
>
> I am the water in my father's eyes
>
> I am the slow flow that takes me gently down.

The sense of loss and isolation become poignant in the absence of his father. He vividly recollects the changes between his time and his father's, between himself and his father:

My old father believes, even in his last days;
That's why he isn't a lover or a poet. ,
He cannot drown himself in water or in awe.
(*A Whiteness of Bone* 2)

In 'Consolations', the poet falls back on the memories of his dying father. He is certain that there is no is escape from past, pain or from death:

I remember my father, dying
under the slackening kindness of Librium,
making pained noises, reaching out
his life to fill my tongue and mouth
with the bitter taste of despair.
The other dead are so quiet.
And one fats no more
than a pressing shadow of shame
when one remembers them. (*A Whiteness of Bone* 4)

He recollects his dead father when he is in deep anguish. The bondage that once was established never breaks down. Even in death, the father shares the son's suffering and sympathizes:

And through the dull suburbs
of his death, my old father
gropes his way back,
yes, he seems to whisper
overwhelmed by the defeat
in my eyes, hunger and death
made the bones of one's breath. (*A Whiteness of Bone* 4)

It is relevant in this context to remember what Mahapatra wrote about his father in an autobiographical and reflective essay:

> My father worked as a sub-inspector of primary schools and his earnings were comparatively meagre father's work kept him away from home. It would be right to say, however, that there was a strong and worm bond between us, father and son, right from the beginning,

> and that this lasted night until his death. That was a little more than two years ago. Besides, perhaps as emotional involvements usually are, something in the way a father reaches for his son's hand, with a vague longing that life should last forever, I remember the web of force the silence of which we are a recognize part. This time protected me with courage. (*Contemporary Author's Autobiography Series* 138)

In 'Orissa Landscape' the poet fondly recollects a moment when he cut his chin and his mother came worried and pressed sugar against the wound to check the flow of blood. For Mahapatra, the blood is not blood, it is the Ooze of love:

> A long time ago
> I cut my chin and bled.
> My mother clumsily held a lump of sugar
> against the wound
> to stop the Ooze of love.
> (*Two Decades of Indian Poetry* 120)

Mahapatra's reverence for past, his allegiance to the tradition and flow of inheritance are so deep-delved that even in misery and helplessness, he sheds warm tears like his 'father's child'(s). When the poet sojourns the galaxy of his familial past, his father, grandfather, mother, younger brother—all twinkle like stars to comfort him in the darkness of the present.

Mahapatra recapitulates the memories of his younger brother and mother:

> To night.
> The shadow of my brother follows me,
> becoming blood on its hooves.
> My loving mother turns pale and crass
> (*A Whiteness of Bone* 3)

He recollects the pain his mother had had to consume. His sympathies with the aged mother make him a silent part of the life lost beyond recall:

In the room of mine
Last year's calendar hangs uselessly on the wall.
In my mother's eyes pain begins to stir again
like a venerable old gentleman
who has returned from afar. (*A Whiteness of Bone* 15)

Sitting alone at a December dawn, the poet recollects his mother and compares his own sadness with his mother's:

The old woman
With a grey hair and coarse wrinkled hands
Whom I call mother looks vacantly into her
Tea cup, thinking she has been betrayed.
(*A Whiteness of Bone* 24)

Remembering the flutter of whiteness and whispers of desolation that surrounded his house and the changed mother; the poet's heart goes dark:

But what I realize is that
before I reach that the door,
it would have turned white.
Mother stands by the door
still wearing her clothes of mourning.
I don't remember what father's death was like.
(*A Whiteness of Bone* 29)

The poet expresses a futile attempt to do away with the past. It may be the fact that the past is the repository of infinite pains and anguishes. He falls back on the house that sheltered him once:

There is a photograph still hanging
on the walls in my father's house. It is quite old,
and against an elaborate backdrop the photographer used
are my parents, my younger brother and I.
I want to shut it from my mind
because it reminds me of a useless monument.
(*A Whiteness of Bone* 29)

With a deep sense of anguish at heart the poet tries to dispossess the past. But his real intention is to protect and preserve the past in the closet of his heart:

> Now with what longings
>
> Shall I protçct my memory? (*A Whiteness of Bone* 43)

Mahapatra's poetry authenticates his reverence for and faith in the post which is deeprooted and redeeming. For Mahapatra, recollection serves as a mode of redemption.

As a complement to and proof of belonging to the past that lies everywhere like water, the poet remembers his old house, his home that housed him once with joy and loneliness. With the passing of time, the willingness to whirl back to infancy becomes stronger:

> This house, my room, yesterday's flowers,
> There are corners my hands never touched.
> Once I touched a woman here,
> her breath warm as too that blows in summer
> who could think thin
> that the lovely body held so much of blood?
> on room's west wall
> the white of a photograph's flight
> has dulled slowly into grimy brown.
> A breath that trembles in a spider-wed there
> could bear witness to my faith in love as memory,
> held as I am love by a fear creeping along the skin.
> Light tricks, revealing unknown bones of the air.
> In the house I figure the possibilities of live. Could I
> hide again as a child, some place here?
> The woman in the silent frame before me
> does not stir, Old murmurs
> wear me out again.
> And I suppose I must have loved.

As I look out, I realize sadly
our sons are with us too. (*House* 22)

The poem is an accurate family album wounded by the force-talons of time with its mute passage. The sadness of the poet stems from the recollection of the lost youth rather than from the presence of two sons who remind of the fast changing patterns of time. Mahapatra's account of the house in his autobiographical essay intensities our understanding of the poet's deep sense of allegiance to it:

> The house where is grew up in Cuttack was locate at one end of a cluster of house—mostly with clay walls and straw-thatched roof—belonging to proper people who liked out their living by doing stray, odd jobs on daily wages (138). The house of my childhood turned into a strange, intense memory in later years. This was the one father built into which we moved when I was nearly six. Father had left for the interior province, and we lived by ourselves alone. The rights were uncertain, fall of the unknown, and I recollect barring the front and back doors without fail before the onset of darkness every evening. A dismal setting indeed, and one which haunted me with certain persistence until years later a day came when I decided to put the whole thing on a paper in an exercise of exorcism.... So this house of mine became substance, as did my mother physically ill with the passage of time, moving back and forth in the listless darkness, my younger brother at his heals. We had no electricity in the house (It was luxury for us), and the long veranda with its adjoining courtyard seemed to float about in a ghostly light, feeling me with a sense of necessity—I could not overcome. (*Contemporary Author's Autobiography*, 140-41)

Mahapatra's whirling back to the place of his birth and childhood has become a passion that keeps him away from the fear of being faceless in this crowded world. In 'December' he makes this passion explicit:

To live one must do those things one loves.
but always in secret. So to keep going

back to the place one has come from.

(*A Whiteness of Bone* 24)

In trying to disown his house, the poet however clings to it intimately:

Once there was more to this than meets my eye;
the beamed roof of the house, the veranda,
the pitchers of waters for as to drink
a lanterns light and rest in some one's eyes
leaving over the night. (*A Whiteness of Bone* 29)

The poet's unblemished love for and reverence to his ancestral familial past constitute a bower for him. The poet's desire that flows down the banks of his ancestral past remains the recurrent motif for him, which revitalizes and authenticates his identity. In "Way of the River", the poet celebrates his identity, following the slow flow of the river across sal and deodar. While ruminating over the private past, the poet fells the greater pull of the place where he was born. He transports himself from the microcosm of private self and through such transportation the poet tries to identify himself with his roots. Groomed as a home bound pilgrim, and without it, he cannot runway from the theme-song of life. Mahapatra's allegiance to the roots is the result of his wholehearted understanding of the place he lives and writes in:

This is the town where I was born: herewith others,
Year after year I celebrate the joyous festivals,
in the whine of the cripple and mangled leper
I see the power of the people holding their ground,
the mystery of the gold of charity. (*Waiting* 27)

these lines depict, the sharp memory of the poet, and show how it enlightens him, enables him to make his life worth living. Memory of his ancestors always haunts him. These memories make his living fruitful and meaningful. The poet writes:

We shall long remember them
the dead, their names,
the peeling stones,

on which dreams grind away
the pale hours. (*Waiting* 16-17)

The memories bridge him with his past and establish a viable rapport with his native land. They intensify the poet's relationship with his roots.

Mahapatra's poetry is replete with images of the reflecting nature of time which is constantly being wounded by the fear of ageing and death, and haunted by the shades of cloudiness, the poet likes to redeem himself through a prayer which will allow him but to link himself to the ancestors and reflect their lost amplitudes. Though if the poet believes in the circular movement of the time around the self, he cannot free himself from the linear expansion of time in which one gets posited in the flux. If in the early poetry Mahapatra's concern walls celebrating the citadel of the private past, in his later poems he has grown conscious of his own time and more particularly the impressions that time leaves on an individual's growth from childhood to old age and death. A poet is the product of a society and culture. His sensibility, attitude and vision get shaped by that society and culture. He has a responsibility not only to come to terms with himself but also with others. Until the point of this realization, the poet becomes a private man and he begins to lose his social relevance. Mahapatra sums up the objective of his later poetry:

> You say (ask) that my poems are sort of private ritual of discovery, relationship and reaching out to others; if there is catharsis in my writing, it comes our involuntarily, of there is a spiralling. So I try to get into the centre of myself I feel I am somehow afraid of this closeness too and I try to move out of the centre of my life. Yes my poems might be a ritual of finding myself first, feeling the beat of the blood in my hand which feels myself. (*The Poetry of Jayanta Mahapatra*)

In one of his early poems, "Performance", Mahapatra depicts his plight in a changing world. He develops a hope of cleansing himself of the impurities and ugliness of the world. He wants to show his sense of insecurity and disease by constantly disappearing into the affairs of his fellow beings. He honestly admits:

I am eager to disappear into the living, once again,
away from the forebodings of mirror or river,
from the unhurried poise that seems to protect me
from the evil, the old glance stone,
If I were young I could have killed myself
for not being loved back, or simply for the right to fall in love,
perhaps
to write poetry with tears and gall
now between the store and the moon my breath cuts the silence in
two, cobwebs hand low over the roads
of a time that is never restored to
its place; (*A Father's Hours* 11)

In spite of the eagerness to disappear into the fabric of living, the poet's sense of isolation deepens and intensifies precisely because of time and the unsavoury changes it brings to him. He becomes conscious of adhering to walls of ageing. He feels that he is being distanced from himself by the movement of time. He is made to realize that time keeps no fidelity. A sense of diffidence eats away his strength. He often feels uncertain about himself and about his friends. He writes:

This is the age wanting to leave me behind;
The time that is left prevents me from speaking,
Because there are things which have nothing in common,
Between us, taking me away from myself,
Because of the time again
(Can time ever know fidelity is?)
That will have had too much of its dream.
(*A Father's Hours* 15)

In 'The twenty-fifth Anniversary of a republic; 1975', Mahapatra painfully portrays the ironical situation that has crept into his own country, effecting his own countrymen. As a poet he thought of changes to happen for better in his country. But the saddened poet confronts a grim and barren world, and visibly he envisions no change of the prevailing situations of injustice, corruptions and indiscipline.

He ruefully writes:

> This is a barren world that has been
> prowling round my room, epidemics in the poisoned air,
> dusty streets stretching away like disgruntled socialists.
> (*A Father's Hours* 11)

He further adds:

> The prostitutes are younger this year
> at the police station they are careless
> to give reasons for being what they are.
> And the older women careful enough not to show their years. (12)

In 'The Lost Children of America', Mahapatra depicts in his characteristic way the peculiarities of the city in which he lives. His understanding of the city, and therefore, his identification with it seems to be total. He catalogues the different faces of the crowed city Cuttack, rampant with diseases, corruption, violence and wound, the poet maintains a paradoxical stance he painfully records:

> Here
> In the dusty malarial lanes
> of Cuttack where years have slowly lost their secrets
> they wander.
> in these lanes nicked by intrigue and rain
> and the unseen hands of Gods
> In front of a garish temple of the Simian Hanuman
> along river banks splattered with excreta rotting tomatoes
> fish-scales and the moist warm odor of bananas and piss

passing by the big-breasted, hard lied young whores
who fragment the empty silent space behind the local cinema
go on delivering their pre-election speeches
and on the high road above the town's burning ground
from which gluttonous tan smoke float up
in the breeze, smacking of scorched marrow and doubt.
(*Life Signs* 23)

A little later in the same poem, Mahapatra uses irony with a view to harping on the foolishness of the young American children who visit India/Orissa in search of peace. In spite of the age-old belief that India is a great country whose spiritual values that can neither be questioned nor objected to, the poet shows decadence and degeneration have infected the spiritual integrity of the people and the place. The Americans who come here for solace and peace and for a new vision are likely to be frustrated because they are to encounter there the burden which they volunteered to escape from in their own country. Mahapatra exposes the symptoms of decadence that are responsible for the withering away of the spiritual values:

The poet writes:

In the Hanuman Temple last night
the priest's pomaded jean-clad son
raped the squint eyed fourteen-year fisher girl
on the cracked stone platform behind the shrine
and this morning her father found her at the police station
assaulted over and over again by four policemen
dripping of darkness and scarlet death. (*Life Signs* 26)

His poetry is the anguished outpourings of an acutely sensitive man. He sees how man has killed his conscience and embraced violence as a norm. The policeman, the guardian of law, instead of providing legal protection, assaulted her again and again. We are the impotent, voiceless, unquestioning and callous father of the girl. Mahapatra's whole oeuvre reveals his extreme sensitivity to the larger issues that concern mankind in general and our society in particular (Satchidanandan 226). In 'The Land that is Not' the poet speaks about the present, between the past and the future, and says:

The land some call holy
is not the one I want to live in.
Today the land of shrines and temples
offers its troubled tombs of blood,
I want the graveyard to flower without its corpses;
and the sunlit street
to shine without its shadows.
I want the flames to warm the empty heart
of love, not burn a city with pitiable hearted.
I want my government to hover
like a butterfly over a garden;
not be, as it is, like a wasp or snake.
I only want to renew myself like this old river's quiet
that has emerged victorious
over a hundred layers of religion
in the airlessness of the dead. (*Random Descent* 70)

Courage, sacrifice, protest and martyrdom seen to be dead. People have not progressed hand in hand with their country after independence. They have buried history, butchered the past idealism. Gandhiji's Ahimsa remains as a dead ideal for the posterity. The head of Mahatma is seen shining on coins that are preserved in the pockets of shrunken classroom children.

In 'A country' the poet carefully portrays the real story of the Indian villages where poverty and hunger conspire to take away whatever is essentially human in the people.

The poet poignantly predicts the situation:

I, too, listen to the faraway wailing of hyenas
aware of the dying countryside around them,

> tortured by hunger and the reek of decay in the airs
> after the age old myths have been told all over again. (30)

Mahapatra is more concerned with the survival of man in this planet. This always makes him write about the affected people and their quest for existence. One can easily identify his social concern from his Bhopal poems. These poems deal with the Bhopal tragedy which took away many lives. "In Monsoon Day Fable", Mahapatra registers his disenchantment with the place he was born. It is a poem that uncovers the inner layer of pretenses and finally the poet's growing sense of aloneness:

> The Cuttack dawn herds the emaciated cows
> towards the municipal slaughter-house, their feet
> slipping, their eyes following the vague light
> into silence. Wet, as though with glue, they hunt
> me through the nights, perhaps equipped with designs
> To show man his true nature, perhaps
> like the eyes of Einstein. For me to deny
> the thought that I am in a sort of exile. (41)

The poetry of Jayanta Mahapatra, on the other hand, discovers in his culture another metaphor for identity. The poet consciously and conscientiously perpetuates his journey within towards the self and even towards the deposits of cultural sediments in the self. In other words, Mahapatra makes attempt to know the multiple forces that contributed to the composition growth and flowering of his own self. Mahapatra's grandfather accepted Christianly out of compelling forces of famine and poverty, and that he is a Christian living in a Hindu dominated society might have generated a feeling of alienation, a sense of insecurity and alienation, Mahapatra in his poetry perpetuates his quest of identity, and he is keen on the assertion of his identity emanating from a veritable part of this holy land and its miraculous traditions.

Mahapatra falls back on the private or personal past and the racial past to authenticate and legitimize his identity. His acceptance of both the forms of the past as the surest proofs against the feeling of rootlessness and alienation which emanate partly from his being a Christian and partly from his choice of English as the creative medium, shows the reflection of his journey within.

Orissa, popularly known as the land of Lord Jagannath, remains at the core of Mahapatra's creativity. In a good number of poems Mahapatra tries to evoke an atmosphere of the land's lost glory and the lost ecstasy of Orissan culture. In Bhubaneswar, the poet juxtaposes two images of the city: First the ruins of the temples and the pervading silence, second the urban squalor, the humdrum of the city life. The poet forever points to the lost historic tradition that embodies permanence of silence and beauty, even amid ruins, the later typifying the modern man's morbid sense of helplessness amid things transitory. Most of Mahapatra's poems illustrate the straying strand of his deep rooted commitments to and involvement with Orissa and its richly endowed cultural heritage. Mahapatra's adherence to the historical, mythical or cultural past stems from his three-tier understanding of time. He believes:

> The physical perspective changes every moment: perhaps, this is what hammers on the self of one's incurrent isolation that time is not constant, and the present is not present any longer. Slowly I realize that I'm living at one particular instant in many layers of time. The mythic, the historical and the present, what I see in the present is only what has stirred the air of the place for countless generations. (*Queer is Quarterly* 70)

It will not be misleading, therefore, to observe that Mahapatra's culture bound vision emerges from his rueful and tragic realization of the fleeting nature of time. He clothes his poetry in and clings to this vision with a view to overcoming the burdens of mortality, the inevitable burdens of ageing, disease, poverty, hunger and death. Such a vision serves as a shield that protects him from losing his face—both physical and linguistic—physical because of his choice of English as the creative medium. It would, perhaps be rewarding to situate Mahapatra's poetry in such and electic perspective. Both as an individual and as a poet, Mahapatra felt the need to share his feelings with others. Such a desire may be the outcome of his assertion of the cultural identity.

He writes:

> A poet is a poet by reason of his invention, by his ability to express his feeling for life. His heart emerges out of the desire to share, to communicate. There is absolutely no sense in a person creating poetry or other art if he is not able to share his thoughts with others. And he must interact in order to grow. ("The Stranger Within" 432)

Thus an in-depth study of Mahapatra's poetry is likely to reveal the vast range of his outlook, the multifarious themes and above all his distinct style. Repetitive use of images, symbols, is an attempt to lull the reader into the realm of mystery, moving suddenly from the descriptive to the deeply reflective mode of expression, and the using the natural world are the means to illustrate his mental landscapes. Mahapatra's uniqueness as an Indian poet writing in English lies in his rootedness. The details of landscape that come out alive in his poetry suggest the voice of a true insider and the true human condition in the honest language of the poet. But, above all, his poetry celebrates his relationship with his home, Orissa, its people, its past and its weather and its environment. In the process, Mahapatra glorifies its life—both dead and alive.

While searching for his roots and identity, the poet celebrates Orissa as his home/motherland. In portraying a realistic picture of poverty, hunger and starvation of his homeland, Mahapatra comes in a close relationship with his family, his fallow and his grandfather. Mahapatra is well aware of the sensibility and aestheticism of home. Home sustains a promise of life. It assumes its value and a metaphoric stance in Mahapatra's life and poetry. By constantly harping on home, family and relationship, Mahapatra relates himself to his home, his land Orissa, and country, its landscape, its history and its milieu.

7
Conclusion

The poets studied in the preceding chapters Ezekiel, Ramanujan, Parthasarathy, Kamala Das and Jayanta Mahapatra,—have proved the worth and authenticity of Indian English poetry in the post-independence era. They have been successful in discovering and maintaining their identities in a language that they have nativized into an indigenous tradition. Each of these poets has moulded and refreshed the English language to suit to his/her purpose, thereby providing the contemporary Indian English poetry a distinct eminence. They have articulated and authenticated their own identities by showing a sense of belonging to and connecting themselves with the place of their birth, the community and moulded its tradition and culture, its language and literature. Their intense sense of belonging to a home, their land and the roots, their immediate response to the contemporary Indian situations around, and the inner urge to evolve in English a native idiom that an Indian speaks, writes and perhaps understands contribute largely to the formation of a home-bound vision.

This sense of belonging to the native place—whether it is Bombay, Madras Malabar or Orissa—shapes the sensibility and vision of these poets. Every place embraces a composite culture. John D. Peters in a seminal study of *The Illustrated Weekly* of India advocates that language and culture are tightly bound together and that language is "imbued with culture and predestines the possible forms of experience" (Peters 3).

Therefore, those poets, in order to reaffirm their ties with the place, establish their rapport with the native language.

Ramanujan and Parthasarathy ransack the cupboard of their private familial past as well as the linguistic traditions. They fall back on a literary tradition moulded by the place. Both Ramanujan and Parthasarathy try to incorporate into their English poetry the forms of classical Tamil and Kannada poetry. Ramanujan cements a close and inseparable tie with the Tamil past at the familial level, and leans on the classical Tamil and Kannada literary traditions on the linguistic level by closely following and imitating the classical literary forms.

Both Ramanujan and Parthasarathy remit and relive their private familial past, which is indicative of their quest for roots. As an expatriate, Ramanujan lived in America but his spirit ever inhabited the Indian subcontinent, his home, the place of his birth. To overcome the burden of alienation and identity-crisis, he reminisces and fails back on his personal and familial past. Parthasarathy's initial with Britain Raj makes him recognize the significance of his roots. His *Rough Passage* shows his commitment to his native tradition and culture. Thus he is able to resolve the problem of identity and alienation by clinging to his roos, thereby reconstructing his home/nation. If Ramanujan suggests a kind of vision for home and reconstruct it, which out of an instinctive awareness of the centrality of familial experiences, Parthasarathy emerges from an inner compulsion to cling to the Tamil roots. In Parthasarathy's poetry, the journey seems to be towards the 'hour glass of Tamil mind' (*Rough Passage* 24) rather than towards the 'exact chronometer of Europe' (24). Both Parthasarathy and Ramanujan take to the ironic mode that help them see the past and their own self objectively and clinically.

Nissim Ezekiel, on the other hand, has no linguistic tradition whosoever to fall back on. English language shaped his sensibility both at home and school. So he does not perpetuate his quest through a linguistic past. Presumably his "backward place" is where he is to-day. His concern is the present—the dialect of the Indian using English. He discovers in Indian English his literary tradition and seeks to revitalize his identity as an Indian. The study of Ezekiel's poems has evinced that he is perpetuating his spiritual quest for home not through the Hindu scriptures but the Bible. In a secular context, religion—Jew or Christian or Hindu—does not pose any problem of identity.

In spite of his Jewish background, Ezekiel's involvement with Bombay—the miniature secular India—is total. His Ben-Israeli origin never stood on his way in developing and cultivating a definable relationship with Bombay in Particular and India in general. Although Ezekiel does not have his roots deep in the Indian Past or its tradition, he develops an intense relationship with the present-day India, its people, its ethos and culture. His verse bold by sings of his total commitment to Bombay and India, the land of his birth.

Being a few, Ezekiel is an outsider to the composite Indian culture, and yet he is recognized as the representative voice of the postcolonial India. Indian writing in English thrived and flourished before Ezekiel, but it was he who pioneered in nativising the language like all postcolonial poets and writers. His poetry shows his commitment to build/construct Indian and reaffirms his Indianness.

He writes:

> The Indian landscape sears my eyes.
> I have become part of it
> To be observed by foreigners
> And
> My backward place is where I am.
> (*Collected Poems* 181)

In "Night of the Scorpion", the poet expresses a sense of distance and alienation as well as the acceptance of love. Ezekiel emphasizes on the Indian culture of tolerance and goes on to justify how human emotions link everything. Home/family and nation are the central metaphors in the work of the poets chosen for study in the present dissertation. Strengthening the bond of familial kinship and recapturing the past values have been their hallmark. In the "Very Indian Poem in Indian English", Ezekiel authenticates his understanding of the way in which Indians use

English. The poet knowingly makes use of present continuous tense and linguistically and grammatically incorrect sentences to show the manner in which Indians are accustomed to using English. In fact, Ezekiel and his art thrive on the strength and validity of Indian background.

Jayanta Mahapatra and Kamala Das are deeply rooted in their soil. Both cling to their native land, its culture and people, its history and tradition. In Mahapatra's poetry, Orissa, the land of his birth, assumes a metaphoric dimension of home through its social, cultural and historical implications. The place is central to his poetic consciousness. The poet not only reiterates his allegiance to the place of his birth, he establishes a rapport with its culture, tradition and heritage of which he is a vital part. Mahapatra not only remembers the glorious past of Orissa's maritime navigators, the social, cultural and religious passions of his people, he also glorifies the art and architecture of the land, the city of Cuttack and Bhubaneswar, the "Black Pagoda" of Konark, the Jagannath of Puri, and the river Daya on whose banks the climactic Kalinga battle of 261 BC was fought with Emperor Ashoka. Mahapatra, by so doing, identifies himself with his land and environment, which helps him search for his self, his roots and his identity. The poet celebrates Orissa as his motherland.

Kamala Das glorifies the values held dear by home, domesticity and family life. She is aware that intimacy of relationship not only binds the family but also serves as a booster to build/construct home/community/nation. She writes about her roots, background and her Nalapat house in Malabar. The Nalapat house in Malabar remains close to her heart and art. Kamala Das's instinctive choice of English as her poet medium does not diminish or hamper her identity, rather it rein forces her distinctiveness and rootedness as an Indian. Her poetry gives vent to the thoughts and feelings of a modern woman from a woman's point to view. Kamala Das's poetry is a truthful and transparent record of her life story, a candid portrayal of her joys and agonies and a persistent quest for herself and her Nair back ground. She tries to find herself through love and relationship and familial ties when she pines to go back to Malabar in search of childhood joy and innocence. Her poems build a strong vision of home/family and evoke the poet's desire to renovate, rebuild and recapture her ancient home, she writes:

When I grow old, I said,
And very very rich
And make new this ancient home.
(*The Old Playhouse and Other Poems* 16)

This book tries to bind the poets—Ezekiel, Ramanujan, Jayanta Mahapatra, Parthasarathy and Kamala Das—in conformity with the visions they share together. Their poetry is home/family/nation bound with a distinctive zeal to rebuild or reconstruct it. Such will and zeal the poets register in the bulk of their poetry vindicate their quintessential postcolonial gesture. Parthasarathy shows his compulsion to cling to the Tamil roots. Ramanujan's vision emerges from an instinctive awareness of the centrality of familial experience. Ezekiel's unflinching commitment to Bombay, the place of his birth, and the dialect of the Indian using English, is the stamp of his poetry. Jayanta Mahapatra's vision evolves out of his realization of being rooted and bound to Orissa, the place where he is born and brought up. Kamala Das's glorification of the values of home, domesticity and family life, and her pining for love, innocence and joy in relationships are definite indicators of her home-bound vision. Home/nation is the beginning and the end of their journey.

It won't be out of place to reiterate that these poets writing in English in the post-independence era have discovered a genuine voice, and indigenous idiom and sensibility to marginalize the centre. For them, English is not just a means of communication but a medium of expression, through which they glorify everything Indian and valorize the myths, tradition, culture and heritage of their native land. All of them show a deep sense of belonging to home/family/nation and passionately respond to the situations around them. In order to recapture and rebuild their home, family and nation, these poets have firmly tightened their lies with their roots, built a rapport with the native language and incorporated the forms of their native linguistic tradition into the their English poetry.

This study would remain incomplete in its scope and dimension if it does not make a reference to a couple other contemporary Indian poets, in whose works Indianness occupies a significant space. Arun Kolatkar and Niranjan Mohanty write with a sense of place. Each of these poets shows an earnestness to remain home-bound, root-bound and family-bound. These poets prove that an indigenous tradition of Indian poetry in English is already formed and they are the product of this tradition.

Arun Kolatkar's *Jejuri* is regarded as a quest poem. It has drawn critical acclaim for its thematic unity and technical vituaosity. The poem, in thirty-six sections, is the outcome of the poet's visit to Jejuri, thirty miles off Pune. With irony, satire and suppleness of insight, the poet has refreshingly portrayed his understanding of the place. Jejuri is a place of pilgrimage, where Khandoba variously known as 'Mallari, Mallari Martand, Mahalaskant, Mailar and Mairal' (Mahadevashastri 613) is worshipped. The poem exposes the poet's skeptical attitude towards the present condition of Jejuri and its gods and deities. Even when the poet is critical and skeptical about Jejuri, she relates himself to the history of the place through his understanding of the legends associated with Khandoba. The two institutions, the temple and the railway station, the one symbolic of the tradition and the other of the contemporary industrial civilization, have been openly attacked because of the lack of affection they show to people who visit them. The callous and selfish priest, the priest's ignorant son, the Station Master, the tea-stall waiter on the platform—all symbolize disaffection and contribute to the steady degeneration taking place in the place of pilgrimage.

King rightly remarks:

> Jejuri is, I think, less a poem of scepticism and
> A poem about a modern wasteland's loss of faith
> Than a poem which contrasts deadness of perception
> With the ability to see the divine in the natural
> vitality of life. (King 170)

What is striking in *Jejuri* is the profoundly ironic vision of the poet who envisages the continuity of life-spirit even amid decadence and sterility and disaffection. Another significant feature which contributes to the greatness of the poem is the casual, informal handling of language. No medium-consciousness obstructs the poet's free play of the image pattern. M. Sivaramkrishna makes and objective study of Kolatkar's handling of the medium. He says:

> And in terms of language and craft there is a muted
> Rejection of the literary element of literature and
> A reliance on imagistic concretion rather than
> Rhetorical description. The ease and casualness
> Of language in Kolatkar is therefore, rooted in the
> Fact that it is denuded of all rhetoric, pared of
> All decorativeness. Objects and experience stand
> Almost naked in the crystalline and denotative purity.
> This purity, while reminiscent of a competent reporter
> In the contemporary context, has its antecedents,
> However, in the folk tradition, which had a seminal
> Significance for our bilingual poets.
> ("The Tongue in English Chains" 243-44)

The dialectical relationship of the poet and the place and the unconventional vision of the 'Bhakti' poet form Kolatkar's home-bound vision.

Niranjan Mohanty (1953-2008), Professor of English, a younger Indian English poet from Orissa is fascinated by the Indian heritage, myths, and legends and contuse. He is firmly rooted in the landscape of his native land Orissa with a primarily rural and romantic sensibility. Mohanty has a deep poet faith in Orissa's culture, its history and religion, Orissan landscapes, contemporaneity, time, data, quest for identity, loneliness, his racial past, devotion, respect for the family and home are the different threads with which he weaves the texture of his poetry (Arora). He paints it with imagery, tonal variations and rhythms. He is perhaps influenced by the poetry of Jayanta Mahapatra and Dylan Thomas. Dr. Sailendra Narayan Tripathy rightly compares Dylan Thomas with Dr. Mohanty:

> Niranjan Mohanty was our Dylan Thomas. Balasore in Orissa was his Swansea in Wales. Both were inspired by T.S. Eliot. Like Thomas, Mohanty's major theme was the unity of all live, a unity out of diversity and he celebrated this unity. Mohanty's Poetry flours from Orissa's folklore. (Tripathy 10)

Mohanty was awarded with International writing Fellow at University of lowa, USA in 1994 and Senior Fellow, Department of Culture, Govt. of India, 1994-97 (*Silencing the Words* 1997), *Oh This Bloody Game!* (1988), *Prayers to Lord Jagannath* (1994), *On Touching You and Other Poems* (1999), *Life Lines* (1999), *Krishna* (2003), *Tiger and Other Poems* (2008) and *A House of Rains* (2008) are the poetic collections that Niranjan Mohanty has left behind him. These poetic volumes prove his worth and identity as a creative artist.

Mohanty's works prove that poetry connects the people. According to him:

> poetry is perhaps a blackboard
> where white whispers of hearts
> get recorded without one's knowledge! (*Touching* 69)

and

> Perhaps language is a river now
> Where I can swim and float any way I like
> Only to get a feel that I'm a part of the tribe.
> (*Prayers to Lord Jagannath* 37)

His poetry, at its best, is a filtration of his humanity, his home-bound vision, as the lines from "Prayers" reveal:

> I know that my English is no English
> The music I seek in the words
> Or in their premeditated silence is not English.
> It's half-Orissan a, half-Indian.
> It gives me the flavours of watered rice

The fragrance of plough—shares and soil.
I choose to write to English, not to go
Beyond the seas, but to meander here
Live the light at the day's end
Among the jasmine whiteness
Of my ancestors. I choose it to make it possession.
My very own, my priceless possession.
(*Prayers to Lord Jagannath* 75)

Mohanty's poetry echoes the harsh realities of modern times. The images of contemporary India emerging from his poetry are colourful and exotic.

Mohanty's poem, "Home", contains 12 small parts which offers a meaning and certain location to home in different manner. For him Home is not simply a house of brick and cement. It is an emotional factor where formality is not adopted a way of live. According to Mohanty "Sweetest and the best all possible nakedness/ is home" (14). So to him possible nakedness—nakedness in nature, nakedness in relation—seems to be sweet. Home is "the beginning and end of sorrows and seas" (14) and at the same time home seems to be "an Indian Air-Hostess" (16).

Oh This Bloody Game!, unfolds different layers of living with a deep-rooted purpose. Loneliness, suffering, obsession with the fear of death are some of the ideas he deals with. Mohanty is a product of the Indian tradition, and he undertakes all the responsibilities that make a man truly Indian. He respects his elders and pays homage to the ancestors.

He states:

With yours I've only learnt
No one loves me without selfishness:
And not even my wife who shares only a part
Of myself, but not myself. (4)

In *Prayers to Lord Jagannath* the poet glorifies the Jagannath culture, Orissan culture—the culture of humbleness. He wishes to live for others:

Only to feed
Those who die of hunger
After flood or bloodshed or drought (*Prayers* 58)

Jagannath culture respects all religion and believes in fate, 'Karma' and 'Dharma'.

He writes:

You already know, Lord,
I am an Indian, an Oriya.
I respect all religions.
I am bound by Karma and Dharma.
I believe in fate. I believe in
Horoscope and palmistry.
And at times I'm Superstitious,
Although I dissected bellies and brains
Of toads and cockroaches, earthworms (*Prayers* 143)

As a humble Orissan, Mohanty believes that the true measures lies not in material pursuit but in spiritual quest of life. He believes on the co-operation, liberty, equality and fraternity which form the spiritual ethos and social fabric of Orissan people.

In *Life Lines* (1999), Mohanty acquaint the readers with the inner self and self beyond, without losing the touch of reality. The use of striking phrases, alliteration, metaphors and similes, Indian words and figures, myths and religion, gives Mohanty's poetry a native flavour. *Krishna* (2003) shows Krishna's love for Radha, but the poem presents the picture of woman's predicament in an orthodox society in which a woman is treated as a second rate creature. The compatible relationship between man and woman, love and dedication, are essential to keep the two bound together.

Krishna and Radha are icons for all men and women who find solution in love. He calls love a human phenomenon, which can be divinized only by living in it.

A House of Rains (2008) Mohanty achieves a distinctive milestone in his poetic journey. In foreword to *A House of*

Rains, he states: "poetry enables me to connect, ennobles and enkindles me to relate myself to a flux that is inescapable, to a centre of faith that is interminable". In an interview to Jaya Deep Sarangi, he states:

> I am spiritual at the core, as a human being, But I am reluctant to go to a temple, always—the rocky ways, the distance, the crowd, the rituals. (*Contemporary Vibes* 27)

Though he never goes to the temple, he envies those who go there.

He writes:

> I never go to temples. I envy
> Those who go. How nicely they go pious
> Ringing the bells, swaying holy flowers
> Perhaps, it's fear—
> The gist of my existence. (*Rains* 74)

On another occasion he writes/asks:

> Which temple shall I visit at day's end,
> For I know not how to pray, what to pray for?
> (*Rains* 119)

The poet in Mohanty hears the sound of prayer in the drops of the rains that patter on his house of rains. He has used 'rain' as metaphor to connect present with past, pleasure wrapped in grief, imagination with reality. He often comes to the house of rains which certainly offers him relief and motivates him to face life.

In the present perspective it is obvious that the Indian poets writing in English today have a definitive and distinctive vision.

Although they have chosen English as their medium of expression, they have already built an indigenous tradition for Indian English poetry so that it may not meander in a haze of uncertainty in future. The word "home" has assumed a deeply metaphoric dimension. This has affected the thematic variety and diversity in the poetry of these writes, and at the same time preserved the unity in terms of the vision embodied in their poetry.

Keki N. Daruwalla sums up:

> The Indian poet tries to give shape and order to his experience and extract some harmony out of the chaos around him. He faces up to his problems and seeks his identity in the country and its incongruities. His concerns may be narrow, but they are almost never trivial. (Daruwalla xxxiv)

The present study evinces that Indian poets' writing in English in the contemporary scenario register a home-bound vision, shaped and moulded by the typical Indian perception of life and reality. They realize the value of love and security a home offers through an understanding of the roots of their existence and the spirit of their milieu. These poets have deftly manipulated English language into the forms to embody the typical Indian ethos, sensibility and attitude. Nissim Ezekiel, A.K. Ramanujan, R. Parthasarathy, Jayanta Mahapatra and Kamala Das are representative Indian English poets of our times, whose quest for home and their zeal to recapture and reconstruct it in all its physical, aesthetic and spiritual dimensions has opened up new avenues and illumined new hopes for the growth of our native tradition in Indian poetry in English.

Bibliography

Abidi, S.Z.H. *Studies in Indo-Anglian Poety*. Bareilly: Prakash Book Depot, 1978.

Abraham, Taisa. *Introducing Postcolonial Theories*. New Delhi: Macmillan Pvt. Ltd., 2007.

Aldan, Daisy. Ed. *Poems from India*. New York: Thomas Y. Crowell, 1969.

——. "Indian Poetry Today," *Books Aboard*, 40:2 (Summer 1966): 397-402.

Alexander, Meena. "Exiled by a Dead Script," *Journal of Indian Writing in English*, 5:2 (1977): 1-4.

Alien, Walter. "Commonwealth Literature," *New Statesman* (10 September 1960): 341.

Ammanuddin, Syed. *World Poetry in English: Essays and Interviews*. New Delhi: Sterling Publishers, 1981.

——. "Trends in Indian Verse in English," *Commonwealth Quarterly*. 1, 4 (September 1977): 1-13.

Amur, G.S. *Images and Impressions*. New Delhi: Panchasheel Prakashan, 1982.

Anand, Mulk Raj. "The Changeling", *Indian Writing in English*. Ed. Ramesh Mohan. Madras: Orient Longman, 1978: 11-20.

Anant, Victor. "The Hypnotized People," *Partisan Review*. 27, 2 (Spring 1960): 311-23.

Anthony, Frank. "English in India: A Historical Appraisal Since 1947," *India and Foreign Review* (1 November 1972): 12-13.

——. "Areas of Promise," *TLS* (24 September 1964): 879.

Arora, Sudhir K. "A Tribute to Prof. Niranjan Mohanty," *Poetcrit*. Vol. XXII (January 2009), No. 1, 113-14.

——. "Niranjan Mohanty: The Poet Who Saw 'Tiger' Everywhere," *Indian Book Chronicle*, 33:10, Oct. 2008: 3-6.

Ashroft, Bill. Gareth Griffiths and Hellen Tiffen. *The Empire Writes Back*. London: Routledge, 1989.

Bains, Y.S. "Review of *The Striders* by A.K. Ramanujan," *Literature East and West*. 11, 1 (March 1967): 72.

Balakrishnan, Purasu. "Contemporary Indian Writing in English," *Triveni*. 47, 3 (October/December 1978): 58-67.

Barua, Dilip K. "Poised Between Two Worlds," *The Statesman: Literary Supplement* (28 February 1982): 1-2.

Belliappa, Meena. "Ezekiel's Poet, Lover, Birdwatcher," *The Miscellany*. 46 (1971): 25-44.

Bhabha, Homi. "Indo-Anglian Attitudes," *Times Literary Supplement* (3 February 1978): 136.

——. *The Location of Culture*. London: Routledge, 1994.

——. "Indo-Anglian Attitudes," *TLS* (21 April 1978): 445.

Bhagat, Dhiren. "Poets: The Limited Clubs," *India Today* (31 July 1982): 131.

Bhatnagar, O.P. "R. Parthasarathy: A Revaluation," *Perspectives*. Ed. B.K. Das, Bareilly: Prakash Book Depot, 1983.

——. Ed. *Studies in Indian Poetry in English*. Jaipur: Rachana Prakashan, 1985.

Birjee Patil, J. "Interior Cadences: The Poetry of Nissim Ezekiel," *The Literary Criterion*. 12, 2-3 (1976): 198-212.

Boehmer, Eleke. *Colonial and Postcolonial Literature*. New Delhi: Oxford University Press, 2005.

Bose, Amalendu. "Some Poets of the Writers Workshop," *Critical Essays on Indian Writing in English*. Ed. M.K. Naik et al. Dharwar: Karnataka University, 1969: 31-50.

——. "New Poetry in India," *Commonwealth Quarterly*. 4, 13 (March 1980): 109-23.

——. "Modern Indian Poetry in English," *Indian Literature*. 13, 1 (March 1970): 51-59.

Broker, Gulabadas. "Projecting the Indian Image," *Quest*. 51 (Dec. 1966): 41-44.

Char, M. Sree Ram. "Secularisation of the Religious Concepts and Idiom in Keki N. Daruwalla's 'Bombay Prayers'," *Poetry*. 12, 1 (1987): 19-31.

Chatterjee, Kalayan K. "Indian English: Problems of Identity," *Quest*. 99 (Jan/Feb 1976): 57-60.

Chaturbedi, P.D. "The Unity of Design in R. Parthasarathy's *Rough Passage*," *Perspectives on the Poetry of R. Parthasarathy*. Ed. B.K. Das. 4-22.

Chaudhury, Nirod C. *To Live or Not to Live*. New Delhi: Orient Paperbacks, 1970.

Chellapan, K. "Ullurai and Iraichi," *Indian Literature*. 30, 1 (Jan/Feb 1978): 70-75.

Chew, Shirley. *The Illustrated Weekly of India*, Encyclopaedia of Literature of Criticism. Ed. Martin Coyle, Peter. Garside, et al. 1990.

——. "London: The most Recent Poems," *The Commonwealth in Canada*. Ed. Uma Parameswaran. Calcutta: Writers Workshop, 1983: 158-73.

Childs, Peter and Patrich Williams. *An Introduction to Postcolonial Theory*. Harvester: Wheatsheat, 1997.

Daruwalla, Keki N. Ed. *Two Decades of Indian Poetry: 1960-1980*. New Delhi: Vikas Publishing House, 1980.

Das, Bijay Kumar. "Aspects of Modern Indian Poetry in English," *The Indian Journal of English Studies*. 20 (1980): 39-50.

——. "Some Indian English Poets of the Severities," *Indian Literature*. 25, 3 (May/June 1982): 101-09.

——. Ed. *Contemporary Indo-English Poetry*, Bareilly: Prakash Book Depot, 1986.

——. Ed. *Perspectives on the Poetry of R. Parthasarathy*. Bareilly: Prakash Book Depot, 1983.

Das, Kamala. *Summer in Calcutta*. New Delhi: Everest Press, 1965.

——. *My Story*. New Delhi: Sterling Publishers Pvt. Ltd., 1976.

——. *Alphabet Lust*. New Delhi: Orient Paperbacks, 1976.

——. *Closure: Some Poems and a Conversation*. New Delhi: HarperCollins Publishers India, 2009.

——. *The Descendants*. Calcutta: Writers Workshop, 1967.

——. *The Old Playhouse and Other Poems*. Madras: Orient Longman Ltd., 1973.

——. *Tonight, This Savage Rite: The Love Poems of Kamala Das and Pritish Nandy*. New Delhi: Arnold-Heinemann (India) Pvt. Ltd., 1979.

Data, Amaresh. "The Other Person," *Indian Literature*. 144 (July/Aug 1991): 95-102.

Datta, Jyotirmoy. "On Caged Chaffinches and Poly Glot Parrots," *Quest*. 28 (Jan/March 1961): 26-32.

Desai, S.K. "Mixing Memory and Desire: Small Scale Reflections on the Poetry of A.K. Ramanujan," *Perspectives on Indian Poetry in English*. Ed. M.K. Naik. New Delhi: Abhinav Publications, 1989: 109-23.

Deshpande, Gauri, Ed. *An Anthology of Indo-English Poetry*. New Delhi: Hind Pocket Book, 1974.

de Souza, Eunice. "Introduction," *To The Unfinished Man* (2nd Edition). Calcutta: Writers Workshop, 1965.

Deswani, Tillotama. Review of Ezekiel's *The Exact Name: The Indian P.E.N.* 35, 5 (May 1966): 179-82.

Devy, G.N. "Alienation as a Means of Self-Exploration: A Study of A.K. Ramanujan's Poetry," *Chandrabhaga* 6 (Winter 1981): 5-19.

——. *After Amnesia: Tradition and Change in Literary Criticism*. New Delhi: Orient Longman Ltd., 1995.

Dimock, Edward C. Jr. *The Literatures of India: An Introduction*. Chicago: The University of Chicago Press, 1974.

Doctor, Geeta. "The Parsi Quartet," *Parsiana* (April/May 1974): 14-21.

Dutta, Ujjall. "Problem of Sex, Self and Art in Nissim Ezekiel's Nudes," *Cygnus*. 2, 1 (1980): 49-57.

——. "Tension Into Poetry: The Case Of R. Parthasarathy," *Perspectives on the Poetry of R. Parthasarathy*. Ed. B.K. Das. Bareilly: Prakash Book Depot, 1983: 16-36.

Dwivedi, A.N. *Indo-Anglian Poetry*. Allahabad: Kitab Mahal, 1979.

——. Ed. *Indian Poetry in English: A Literary History and Anthology*. New Delhi: Arnold-Heinemann, 1980.

——. Ed. *Studies in Contemporary Indo-English Verse: A Collection of Critical Essays on Male Poets*. Bareilly: Prakash Book Depot, 1984.

——. Ed. *Studies in Contemporary Indo-English Verse: A Collection of Critical Essays on Female Poets*. Bareilly: Prakash Book Depot, 1984.

Eng. OOi Boo. "Indian Poets and The Use of English," *Journal of Commonwealth Literature*. 9, 1 (August 1974): 10-19.

Enright, D.J. "Modern Indian Writing," *The Miscellany.* 28 (1968): 61-74.

Ezekiel, Nissim. *A Time to Change*. London: Fortune Press, 1952.

——. "What is Indian in Indo-English Poetry," *Critical Responses: Commonwealth Literature*. New Delhi: Sterling Publisher Pvt. Ltd., 1993.

——. "Culture, Colonialism and Indo-English Poetry," *The Writer as Historical Witness: Studies in Commonwealth Literature*. Ed. Edwin Thirukandial. Singapore: Unipress, 1995.

——. *Collected Poems*. New Delhi: Oxford University Press, 1989.

——. *Hymns in Darkness*. New Delhi: Oxford University Press, 1976.

——. *Latter-Day Psalms*. New Delhi: Oxford University Press, 1982.

——. *Sixty Poems*. Bombay, 1953.

——. *The Exact Name*. Calcutta: Writers Workshop, 1960.

——. *The Third*. Bombay: The Strand Bookshop, 1959.

——. *The Unfinished Man*. Calcutta: Writers Workshop, 1960.

Gandhi, Leela. *Postcolonial Theory: A Critical Introduction*. Edinburg University Press, 1998.

Garman, Michael. "Nissim Ezekiel: Pilgrimage and Myth," *Journal of South Asian Literature*. 11, 2-3 (1977): 209-22.

Gemmil, Janet, "An Attempt To Encompass It All," *Mahfil*. 8, 4 (Winter 1972): 95-100.

Gokak, V.K. *An Integral View of Poetry: An Indian Perspective*. New Delhi: Abhinav Publications, 1975.

——. "The Concept of Indianness With Reference To Indian Writing In English," *Indian Writing in English*. Ed. Ramesh Mohan. Madras: Orient Longman, 1978: 21-25.

——. *Studies in Indo-Anglian Poetry*. Bangalore: Sai Rattan Agency, 1972.

——. Ed. *The Golden Treasury of Indo-Anglian Poetry*. New Delhi: Sahitya Akademi, 1970.

Gowda, H.H. Anniah, "A Defence of Indian Verse in English," *Literary Half-Yearly*. 9, 2 (1968): 23-36.

——. "Contemporary Creative Writers in English in India," *Literary Half-Yearly*. 10, 1 (1969): 17-39.

——. "The Current State of Indian Writing in English," *Literary Half-Yearly*. 12, 2 (1971): 15-20.

——. "The Use of Images in Contemporary Indian Verse in English," *World Literature Written in English*. 20 (November 1971): 61-76.

Gupta, G.S.B. "Some Reflections on Indian Writing in English," *Journal of Indian Writing in English*. 1, 2 (July 1973): 53-60.

Gupta, Rameshwar, "The Indian Writers' Responsibility," *Journal of Indian Writing in English*. 1, 1 (January 1973): 74-78.

Guptara, Prabhu S. "Review of *Selected Poems* by A.K. Ramanujan," *World Literature Today*. 52, 2 (Spring 1978): 344.

Harrex, S.C. "Small-Scale Reflections on Indian English-Language Poetry," *Journal of Indian Writing in English*. 8, 1-2 (January/July 1980): 137-66.

Harrison, Keith, et al. "Khushwant Singh on Language and Literature: An Interview," *World Literature Written in English*. 18 (November 1970): 27-32.

Hess, Linda. "Post Independence Indian Poetry in English," *Quest*. 49 (April/June 1966): 28-38.

——. "India's Search for Self-Expression," *Times Literary Supplement* (10 August 1962): 584-85.

——. "Indo-English Literature," *World Literature Written in English*. Newsletter (April 1967): 3-5.

Hookers, William. "Creative Writing in India," *Triveni*. 37, 1 (April 1968): 62-67.

——. "India's Search for Self-Expression," *Times Literary Supplement*. (10 August 1962), 626.

Iredale, Roger. "R. Parthasarathy: Images of a Poet," *Tenor* 1 (June 1978): 20-22.

——. "Indian Poetry in English Today," *Quest*. 98 (November/ December 1975): 72-74.

Ireland, Kevin. "Review of *The Striders* by A.K. Ramanujan," *Journal of Common Wealth Literature*. 4 (December 1967): 141-42.

Iyengar, K.R. Srinivasa. *Indian Writing in English: Contemporary Indian Literature Series*. Bombay: P.E.N. Centre, 1957.

——. "A Faith That Stumbles, Revives and Endures", *Indian Literature*. 34, 4 (July-August 1991): 78-91.

——. "The Role of The Writer and Critic Today," *Indian Literature*. 18, 1 (January-March 1973): 31-41.

——. *Indo-Anglian Literature*. Bombay: International Book House, 1943.

——. *Two Cheers for the Commonwealth*, Bombay: Asia Publishing House, 1962.

——. *Indian Writing in English*. Bombay: Asia Publishing House, 1962.

Jaggi, Satya Dev. "Indo-English Poetry in the Context of World Standards," *Journal of Indian Writing in English*. 1, 1 (January 1973): 35-38.

Jainapur, S.G. "A.K. Ramanujan," *Poetry, Culture and Language: Indo-Anglian Poets from Karnataka*. Calcutta: Writers Workshop, 1987: 108-40.

Jeffares, A.N. "Introduction," *Common Wealth Literature*. Ed. John Press. London: Heinemann Education Books, 1965, XI-XVIII.

——. "The Study of Common Wealth Writing," *World Literature Written in English Newsletter*. 15 (April 1969): 1-15.

Jones, Joseph. *Terranlia: The Case for English as World Literature*. New York: Twayne Publishers, 1965.

Joshi, K. and S.S. Rao. *Studies in Indo-Anglian Literature*. Bareilly: Prakash Book Depot, India.

——. *Journal of South Asian Literature*. 11, 3-4 (Spring/Summer 1976).

Jussawalla, Adil, Ed. *New Writing in India*. Harmondsworth: Middlesex: Penguin Books, 1974.

——. "The New Poetry," *Journal of Commonwealth Literature*. 5 (1967): 65-78.

Kachru, Braj B. *The Indianization of English: The English Language in India*. New Delhi: Oxford University Press, 1984.

Karen, Smith. "A Study of Arun Kolatkar's Jejuri," *Commonwealth Quarterly*. 3, 12 (September 1979): 20-32.

Karnani, Chetan. *Nissim Ezekiel*. New Delhi: Arnold Heinemann, 1974.

——. "The Poetry of Nissim Ezekiel: A Brief Overview," *Journal of South Asian Literature*. 11, 2-3 (1976): 223-28.

Kher, Indernath. "That Message From Another Shore: The Aesthetic Vision of Nissim Ezekiel," *Mahfil*. 8, 4 (1972): 17-28.

——. "Introduction," *Journal of South Asian Literature*. 11, 2-3 (1976): 3-7.

Khullar, Ajit. "On Indo-Anglian Writing," *Thought*. Vol. 27. No. 2 (11 January 1975): 18-19.

——. "Indo-Anglian Poetry has an Address." *Thought*. 25, 50 (5 December 1973): 17-18.

King, Bruce. *Literature of the World in English*. London: Routledge and Kegan Paul, 1974.

——. "Indian English Poetry Today," *The Literary Half-Yearly*. 26, 2 (1985): 2-13.

——. *Modern Indian Poetry in English*. New Delhi: Oxford University Press, 1987.

Kohli, Devendra. "Passionate Sincerity in Indian Poetry in English," *Journal of Common Wealth Literature*. 9, 1 (August 1974): 20-34.

——. "Landscape and Poetry," *Journal of Common Wealth Literature*. 13, 3 (April 1979): 54-70.

Kohli, Suresh. "Nissim Ezekiel: Pursuit of Perfection," *Indian and Foreign Review*. 8, 9 (May 1971): 15-16.

——. "Indian Poetry in English", *The Indian Literary Review*. 1, 7-8 (November/December 1978): 33-40.

——. Ed. *Aspects of Indian Literature: The Changing Pattern*. New Delhi: Vikash Publishing House, 1975.

Kolatkar, Arun, *Jejuri*. Bombay: Clearing House, 1976.

Kotoky, P.C. *Indo-English Poetry: A Study of Aurobindo and Four Others*. Guwahati: Guwahati University, 1969.

Kulshrestha, Chirantan. "The Self in Ramanujan's *Poetry*", *The Indian Journal of English Studies*. 18 (1978-79): 108-19.

——. "English Verse in India: Some Obstinate Questions," *Contemporary Indian English Verse: An Evaluation*. New Delhi: Arnold Heinemann, 1980: 9-19.

——. "Half-Baked Thoughts on The Unhoused Muse," *The Literary Criterion*. 17, 1 (1982): 67-74.

——. Ed. *Contemporary Indian English Verse: An Evaluation*. New Delhi: Arnold Heinemann, 1980.

Kumar, Shiv K. "Poster-Prayers of Nissim Ezekiel," *Journal of South Asian Literature*, II, 3-4 (Spring/Summer 1976): 263-64.

Kumarappa, B. Ed. *The Indian Literatures of Today: A Symposium*. Bombay: The International Book House, 1947.

Lal, P. "A Few...." *The Unfinished Man*. Calcutta: Writers Workshop, 1960.

——. Ed. *Modern Indian English: An Anthology and a Credo*. Calcutta: Writers Workshop, 1969.

——. "Indian Writing in English," *Harvard Educational Review*. 34, 2 (1964): 316-19.

——. "Indian Writing in English," *India and Foreign Review*. (15 February 1971): 16.

——. "Indian Writing in English," *Quest*. 29 (April/June 1961): 83-86.

——. "Nostalgia Indo-Anglisa," *Journal of Indian Writing in English*. 3, 1 (January 1975): 13-15.

Lall, Emmanuel Narendra. *The Poetry of Encounter: Three Indo-Anglian Poets: Dom Moraes, A.K. Ramanujan and Nissim Ezekiel*. New Delhi: Sterling Publishers Pvt. Ltd., 1983.

Lal, Vinay. "A No Mean Poet of the Mean," *Indian Literature*. 34, 4 (July/August 1991): 158-67.

Madhavan, R. "For Whom Do We Write?" *The Literary Criterion*. 12, 2-3 (1979): 16-20.

Mahapatra, Himansu. *In Memorium, Poesies Indian International*. Ed. S.N. Tripathy. Vol. 44 and 45, 2009.

Mahapatra, Jayanta. *Close The Sky, Ten By Ten*. Calcutta: Dialogue Publication, 1971.

——. *A Father's Hours*. Calcutta: United Writers, 1976.

——. *A Rain of Rites*. Athens: The University of Georgia Press, 1976.

——. *Dispossessed Nest*. Jaipur: Nirab Publication, 1986.

——. *Life Signs*. New Delhi: Oxford University Press, 1983.

——. *Relationship*. Cuttack: Chandrabhaga Society, 1981.

——. *Svaymvar and Other Poems*. Calcutta: Writers Workshops, 1971.

——. *The False Start*. Bombay: Clearing House, 1980.

——. *Burden of Waves and Fruit*. Washington D.C.: Three Continents Press, 1986.

——. *Waiting*. New Delhi: Sam Kaleen Prakashan, 1979.

——. "The Inaudible Response in English Poetry in India." *The Literary Criterion*. 15.1 (1980): 27-36.

——. *A Whiteness of Bone*. New Delhi: Viking, 1982.

——. *Random Descent*. Bhubaneswar: Third Eye Communication, 2005.

——. *Temple*. Sydney: Dangaroo Press, 1989.

——. *The Shadow Space*. Kottayam: D.C. Books, 1997.

——. "The Voice in The Ink," *The Illustrated Weekly of India*. (1 April 1990): 28-30.

Mahashabde, N.C. "Indian Poetry in English," *Quest*. 50 (July/September 1966): 110.

Malik, Keshav. "Review of *Hymns in Darkness*, By Nissim Ezekiel," *Youth Times*. (March 18-31, 1971): 53.

Mc Cord, Howar. "A Letter," *Quest*. 51 (October/December 1966): 110.

Mccutchion, David. *Indian Writing in English: Critical Essays*. Calcutta: Writers Workshop, 1969.

——. "Must Indian Poetry in English Always Follow England?" *Critical Essays on Indian Writing in English*. Ed. M.K. Naik, et al. Dharwar: Karnataka University, 1968, 152-61.

Mcleod, Johan. *Beginning Postcolonialism*. Manchester: Manchester University Press, 2000.

Mehrotra, Arvind K. "The Emperor Has No Clothes," *Chandrabhaga*. 3 (Summer 1980): 17-27.

——. "The Emperor Has No Clothes," *Chandrabhaga*. 7 (Summer 1982): 1-32.

Melwani, Murli Das. *Themes in Indo-Anglian Literature*. Bareilly: Prakash Book Depot, 1977.

Memmi, Albert. *The Colonizer and The Colonized*. Proston: Beacon Press, 1965.

Mirza, Taqui Ali. "A.K. Ramanujan's 'Particular Hell,'" *Indian Poetry in English: A Critical Assessment*. Ed. V.A. Shahane and M. Sivaramkrishna. New Delhi: Macmillan and Co. Ltd., 1980, 152-61.

Mishra, Rabi S. "A.K. Ramanujan: A Point of View", Review of A.K. Ramanujan's *Selected Poems*. *Chandrabhaga* 1 (Summer 1979): 60-66.

Mishra, Soubhagya. "Ezekiel: An Estimation," *Gray Book*. 1, 1 (1972): 18-27.

Mohan, Ramesh. Ed. *Indian Writing in English*. Madras: Orient Longman, 1978.

Mohanty, Niranjan. "The Theme-Song of Life: Poetry of Jayanta Mahapatra," *Contemporary Indo-English Poetry*. Ed. B.K. Das. Bareilly: Prakash Book Depot, 1986, 64-86.

——. "Chicago and AKR", *Indian Literature*. (July/August), Vol. 37, No. 4, 1994.

——. "Rain Poems of Mahapatra: A Study," *Punjab University Research Bulletin*. Vol. XXII, No. 2, October 1991.

——. "Trends in Indian Poetry in English", *Indian English Poetry: Critical Perspectives*. New Delhi: Sarup and Sons, 2004.

——. *Krishna*. Bhubaneswar: Avanti, 2003.

——. *Oh, This Bloody Game!* Berhampur: Poetry Publications, 1988.

——. *Prayers to Lord Jagannath*. New Delhi: HarperCollins, 1988.

——. *The Alien Insiders Literary Notes: A Writers Workshop*. Grey Bird Book, 1978.

——. *Tiger and Other Poems*. New Delhi: Sarup and Sons, 2008.

——. "Patterns of Awareness: A Study in Relationship," *Literati*. 15, 1-2 (June/December 1989): 44-56.

——. "Relationship: A Study," *Poetry*. 10 (1985): 24-40.

——. "Roots Rapture: Poetry of Jayanta Mahapatra," *Literary Horizons*. 2, 1 (1987): 60-61.

——. "Sex, Power and Beyond: A Study in The Poetry of Jayanta Mahapatra," *The Quest*. 1, 1 (March 1987): 37-54.

——. "Voices Behind The Wheel: Poets from Orissa Writing in English," *Indian English Writing*. Ed. R.K. Singh. New Delhi: Bahri Publications, 1987: 59-83.

——. *A House of Rains*. Kolkata: Cambridge, 2008.

——. Ed. *The Golden Voices: Poets from Orissa Writing in English*. Berhampur: Poetry Publications, 1986.

——. *Life Lines*. Kolkata: Cambridge, 1999.

——. *On Touching You and Other Poems*. Kolkata: Cambridge, 1999.

Moraes, Dom F. "Indian Writing in English," *The Onlooker*. (24 June 1976): 32.

Mukherjee, M. Ed. *Considerations: Twelve Studies on Indo-Anglian Writing*. New Delhi: Allied Publishers, 1977.

Nabar, Vrinda. "Review of A.K. Ramanujan's *Selected Poems*," *World Literature Written in English*. 18, 2 (Nov. 1978): 545-47.

——. "Arun Kolatkar: A Bi-Lingual Poet," *World Literature Written in English*. 16, 2 (Nov. 1977): 368-75.

Nagarajan, S. "A.K. Ramanujan," *Contemporary Indian Poetry in English*. Ed. Salem Peeradina. Bombay: Macmillan Co., 1972: 18-21.

——. "Nissim Ezekiel," *Contemporary Poets*. Ed. James Vinson, New York: St. Martin's Press, 1975: 466.

——. "Review of Indian Poetry in English: A Critical Assessment," Eds. V.A. Shahane and M. Sivaramkrishna. *Indian Book Chronicle*. (1 June 1981): 189-91.

——. "Review of *Two Decades of Indian Poetry: 1960-1980*," Ed. Keki N. Daruwalla. Indian Book Chronicle. (1 April 1980). Vol. 5, No. 4: 116-17.

——. "The Indianness of Indian Poetry in English," *Journal of Indian Writing in English*. 1, 2 (July 1973): 1-7.

——. "The Two Worlds of Imagery," *The Poetry of Jayanta Mahapatra*. Ed. M. Prasad. New Delhi: Sterling Publishers Pvt. Ltd., 1986: 98-114.

——. Ed. *Aspects of Indian Writing in English*. New Delhi: Macmillan and Co., 1979.

——. Ed. *Indian Response to Poetry in English*. Bombay: Macmillan and Co., 1970.

——. "Review of *Indian Poetry in English: A Literary History and Anthology*," Ed. A.N. Dwivedi. *Indian Book Chronicle*. Vol. 5, No. 4 (1 April 1980): 115-16.

Naik, M.K. "Echo and Voice in Indian Poetry in English," *Indian Writing Today*. 4, 1 (Jan/March 1970): 32-41.

Naik, M.K. et al. *Critical Essays on Indian Writing in English*. Dharwar: Karnataka University, 1972, 1977.

——. *A History of Indian English Literature*. New Delhi: Sahitya Akademi, 1982.

——. *Dimensions of Indian English Literature*. New Delhi: Sterling Publishers Pvt. Ltd., 1984.

——. Ed. *Perspectives on Indian Poetry in English*, New Delhi: Abhinav Publications, 1984.

——. *Studies in Indian English Literature*. New Delhi: Sterling Publishers Pvt. Ltd., 1987.

Nandakumar, Prema. *Indian Writing in English*, 1972-1973.

——. "English: A Piquant Effect," *Indian Literature*. 9, 4 (October/December 1966): 25-33.

——. "English: Lyricists Lead," *Indian Literature*. 10, 4 (October/December 1967): 9-19.

——. "Indian Writing in English," *Indian Literature*. 20, 4 (July/August 1977): 95-108.

Nandy, Ashis. *The Intimate Enemy: Loss and Recovery of Self Under Colonialism*. New Delhi: Oxford University Press, 1989.

Nandy, Pritish, Ed. *Indian Poetry in English 1947-1972*. Calcutta: Oxford and Ibh Publishing Co., 1972.

——. Ed. *Indian Poetry in English*. New Delhi: Sterling Publishers Pvt. Ltd., 1973.

——. "Indian Poetry in English: The Dynamics of New Sensibility," *Indian Literature*. 14, 1 (March 1971): 9-19.

——. "Review of Two Decades of Indian Poetry: 1960-1980," Ed. K.N. Daruwalla. *Sunday* (1 June 1980): 44-45.

——. Ed. *Indian Poetry in English*. New Delhi: Sterling Publishers Pvt. Ltd., 1973.

——. Ed. *Stranger Time: An Anthology of Indian Poetry in English*. New Delhi: Hind Pocket Books, 1977.

Narasimhaiah, C.D. "Indian Writing in English: An Area of Promise", *Journal of Commonwealth Literature*. 9, 1 (August 1974): 35-49.

——. "Indian Writing in English: A Reply to Dom Moraes," *The Literary Criterion*. 12, 2-3 (1976): 6-15.

——. "Indian Writing in English: An Introduction," *Journal of Commonwealth Literature*. 5 (July 1968): 3-15.

——. et al. "A Symposium on The Writer and The Public," *The Literary Criterion*. 5, 4 (Summer 1963): 42-45.

——. *Indian Literature of The Past Fifty Years (1917-1967)*. Mysore: Mysore University Press, 1970.

——. *The Swan and The Eagle*. Shimla: Indian Institute of Advanced Studies, 1969.

Narayan, R.K. "English in India: The Process of Transmutation," *Some Aspects of Indian Writing in English*, Ed. Naik. Bombay: Macmillan and Co., 1979: 21-23.

Narayan, Shyamala A. "Review of *Hymns in Darkness* by Nissim Ezekiel," *World Literature Today*. 52, 1 (Winter 1978): 177-78.

——. "Review of *Ten Twentieth Century Indian Poets*," Ed. R. Parthasarathy. *World Literature Today*. 52, 1 (Winter 1978): 180.

Padhi, Bibhu Prasad. "The Parallel Voice: A Study of The New English Poetry in India," *Quest*. 98 (November/December 1975): 39-46.

Paniker, K. Ayyappa. "Interview," *Tenor* 2 (Jan 1979): 6-24.

——. "Four Voices and A Medium," *Indian Book Chronicle*. 2, 11 (1 June 1977): 190-91.

——. "Indian Poetry in English and The Indian Aesthetic Tradition," *Indian Journal of English Studies*. 23 (1983), 136-51.

——. "Peacocks-Among Patriarchs: A Close Look at Indian Poetry in English," *New Quest*. 2 (August 1977): 59-70.

——. "The Poetry of Jayanta Mahapatra," *Osmania Journal of English Studies*. 13, 1 (1977): 117-38.

Parker, Michal and Roger Starkey. *Postcolonial Literatures: A Selection of Critical Essays*. New Case Book Series, Chennai: Macmillan Press, 2007.

Parthasarathy, R. "Whoring After English Gods," *Perspectives*, Ed. S.P. Bhagat. Bombay: Popular Prakashan, 1970: 43-60.

——. "Indian English Verse: The Making of a Tradition," *The Humanist Review*. 1, 1 (July/September 1979): 5-8.

——. "Rough Passage." (Notes on Making of a Poem), *Indian Poetry in English*. Hari Mohan Prasad (Ed). Aurangabad: Parimal Prakashan, 1983.

——. "The Exile as Writer: On Being an Indian Writer in English," *The Journal of Commonwealth Literature*. Vol. 13. No. 1, 1977.

——. Ed. *Ten Twentieth Century Indian Poets*. New Delhi: Oxford University Press, 1976.

——. *Rough Passage*. New Delhi: Oxford University Press, 1979.

——. "Foregrounding as an Interpretive Device in Nissim Ezekiel's *Night of The Scorpion*," *The Literary Criterion*. 11, 3 (Winter 1974): 38-44.

——. "How It Strikes Contemporary: The Poetry of A.K. Ramanujan," *The Literary Criterion*. 12, 2-3 (1976): 187-97.

——. "Indo-Anglian Attitudes," *Times Literary Supplement*. (10 March 1978): 285.

——. "Letter to The Editor," *Chandrabhaga*. 2 (1979) 66. 11, 4 (Summer 1975): 26-36.

——. "Tradition and Freedom," *The Indian Journal of English Studies*. 21 (1981-82): 47-59.

Patil, Brije J. "Interior Cadence: The Poetry of Nissim Ezekeil." Vol. 12, No. 2-3, 1976, 198-212.

Patke, Rajeev S. *Postcolonial Poetry in English*. New Delhi: Oxford University Press, 2007.

Peeradina, Saleem. Ed. *Contemporary Indian Poetry in English: An Assessment and Selection*. Bombay: Macmillan and Co., 1972.

Peters, John D. "Some American Reflections on Indian Literature in English," *Journal of Indian Writing in English*. 14, 1-4 (January 1986): 1-16.

Prasad, Madhusudan. Ed. *The Poetry of Jayanta Mahapatra: A Critical Study*. New Delhi: Sterling Publishers Pvt. Ltd., 1986.

——. Ed. *Living Indian English Poets*. New Delhi: Sterling Publishers Pvt. Ltd., 1989.

Prasad, Mohan V. "A Note on Recent Indo-Anglian Poetry," *The Two-Fold Voice*. Ed. D.V.K. Raghavacharyulu. Guntur: Navodaya Publishers, 1971: 127-35.

Press, John. Ed. *Commonwealth Literature: Unity and Diversity in a Common Culture*. London: Heinemann Educational Books, 1965.

Punekar, Shankar M. *Indo-Anglian Creed and Allied Essays*. Calcutta: Writers Workshop, 1972.

Puthuceary, Rosaly. "A Study of *Rough Passage*," *Perspectives on R. Parthasarathy*. Ed. B.K. Das. 31-39.

Raffle, Burton. "Review of *The Striders* by A.K. Ramanujan," *Mahfil*. 3, 2-3 (1966): 85-88.

Raghavacharyulu, D.V.K. *The Two-Fold Voice: Essays on Indian Writing in English*. Guntur: Navodaya Publishers, 1971.

Rahman, Anisur. *Form and Value in The Poetry of Nissim Ezekiel*. New Delhi: Abhinav Publications, 1981.

——. *Expressive From in The Poetry of Kamala Das*. New Delhi: Abhinav Publications, 1981.

Rajiva, Stanley F. "Contemporary Indian Writing in English," *Quest*. 60 (January/March 1969): 72-75.

Rajkumar. "A New Language for New India: A Utopian Dream," *Punjab University Research Bulletin* (Arts). 3, 2 (October 1972): 267-78.

Rajyalakshmi, P.V. *The Lyric Spring*. New Delhi: Abhinav Publications, 1977.

Ramakrishna, E.V. "Parthasarathy's Self-World: A Reading of *Rough Passage*," *Perspectives on the Poetry of R. Parthasarathy*. Ed. B.K. Das. Bareilly: Prakash Book Depot, 1983: 52-60.

Raman, A.S. "India: Mukherjee to Banerjee," *London Magazine*. 14, 3 (August/September 1974): 117-23.

Ramanujan, A.K. "Talking to God in the Mother Tongue," *Manushi*. (Jan-Jun) No. 50-52: 9-14, 1989.

——. *The Striders*. London: Oxford University Press, 1966.

——. "A Meeting," *Thought*. 21, 48 (Nov. 29, 1969): 11-13.

——. *Relations*. London: Oxford University Press, 1971.

——. *Second Sight*. New Delhi: Oxford University Press, 1986.

——. *Selected Poems*. New Delhi: Oxford University Press, 1976.

——. *Speaking of Siva*. Harmondsworth: Penguin, 1973.

——. *The Collected Poems*. New Delhi: Oxford University Press, 1995.

——. *The Interior Landscape*. Harmondsworth: Penguin, 1970.

——. *Uncollected Poems and Prose*. Eds. Molly Daniels-Ramanujan and Keith Harrison. New Delhi: Oxford University Press, 2001.

Ranjan, B. "Remarks on Identity and Nationality," *Literature East and West*, 9, 2 (1965): 90-60.

——. "India," *Literature of the World in English*. Ed. Bruce King. London: Routledge and Kegan Paul, 1974: 79-97.

——. "The Indian Virtue," *Journal of Commonwealth Literature*. 1 (September 1965): 79-85.

Rao, C. Sibha and D. Kesava Rao. "R. Parthasarathy: Compact With Silence: A Study of Rough Passage," *The Literary Criterion*. 23, 4 (1988): 42-48.

Rao, K. Raghevendra. "Indo-Anglian Writers," *Quest*. 29 (April/June 1961): 116.

——. "Foreword to Kanthapura," Madras: Oxford University Press, 1974.

——. "Reverse Romanticism: The Case of A.K. Ramanujan's *The Striders*," *Aspects of Indian Writing in English*. Ed. M.K. Naik. Delhi: Macmillan and Co., 1979: 120-25.

——. "The Predicament of Indo-English Poet: A Retrospect and Prospect," *Journal of Literature and Aesthetics*. 1, 2 (March 1981): 31-68.

Rao, P. Mallikarjun. "The Poetry of Exile: A Study of A.K. Ramanujan," *Kakatiya Journal of English Studies*. 5 (1983).

Rao, Raja. "The Climate of Indian Literature Today," *The Literary Criterion*. 10, 3 (1972): 1-7.

Rao, Vepa. "Review of Alphabet of Lust" in *The Hindustan Times Weekly* (Sunday, July 17, 1977).

Rath, Harihar. "Parthasarathy's *Rough Passage*: Vision and Attitude," *Perspectives on the Poetry of R. Parthasarathy*. Ed. B.K. Das. Bareilly: Prakash Book Depot, 1983.

Rayan, Krishna. "Edinuburgh and The Indian Experience," *The Sunday Observer*. 17 (June 1984): 15.

Rodrigues, Santan. "An Interview With Nissim Ezekiel," *Youth Times*. (1-14 February 1980): 17. Vol. 8, No. 17.

Rose, Aileen D. *The Hindu Family in Its Urban Setting*. Toronto: University of Toronto Press, 1961.

Rose, Raul D'gama. "So Much Light in Total Darkness," *Review of Hymns in Darkness*. Kavi (Jan 1975): 32-35.

Sabherwal, V.J. "Good Wine and Some Cobwebs," Review of Nissim Ezekiel by Chetan Karnani. *Indian Book Chronicle* (1 July 1976): 193-95.

Saha, Subhas C. *Modern Indo-Anglian Love Poetry*. Calcutta: Writers Workshop, 1971.

——. "Ezekiel's Enterprise," *The Miscellany*. 40 (July/August 1970): 10-23.

——. "Indo-Anglian Verse: A Comic Attitude," *Thought*. (22 March 1969): 15-16. Vol. 21, No. 11.

——. "Review of The Unfinished Man," *Thought*. 40, 21 (December 1969): 16-18.

——. "Search for Indianness in Writing," *India and Foreign Review*. (15 March 1976): 8-9. Vol. 13, No. 6.

Satyanarayana, M.R. "Jejuri: Arun Kolatkar's Wasteland," *Osmania Journal of English Studies*. 13, 1 (1977): 201-16.

Sergent, Howarde. Ed. *Pergamon Poets: Poetry from India*. Oxford: Pergamon Press, 1970.

——. *New Voices of The Commonwealth*. London: Evans Brothers, 1968.

Shahane, Vasant A. and M. Sivaramakrishna. Eds. *Indian Poetry in English: A Critical Assessment*. New Delhi: Macmillan and Co., 1980.

Shahane, Vasant A. "The Religious-Philosophical Strain in Nissim Ezekiel's *Poetry*," *Journal of South Asian Literature*. 11, 3-4 (Spring/Summer 1976): 253-61.

Shaligram, Ruta. "The Family in Modern Indian English Poetry," *The Indian P.E.N.* (April-June 1991): 8-10.

Sharma, K. Godavari. "The Poetry of R. Parthasarathy," *Perspectives on the Poetry of R. Parthasarathy*, Ed. B.K. Das. 61-70.

Sharpe, Patricia H. "The Plight of The Indian Writer Today," *Quest*. 59 (October/December 1968): 31-39.

——. "Review of *Modern Indian Poetry in English: An Anthology and a Credo*," Ed. P. Lal. *Mahfil*. 8, 4 (Winter 1972): 101-11.

Sidhanta, N.K. "English," *The Indian Literatures of Today: A Symposium*. Ed. B. Kumarappa. Bombay: The International Book House, 1947.

Singh, Amarjit, "Contemporary Indo-English Literature: An Approach," *Aspects of Indian Writing in English*. Ed. M.K. Naik. Delhi: Macmillan and Co., 1979: 1-14.

Singh, Brijraj. "An Admirable Curtain Raiser," Review of Ten Twentieth-Century Indian Poets, Ed. R. Parthasarathy. *Indian Book Chronicle.* (16 July 1977), 241-45. Vol. 3, No. 7.

——. "Journey Into Self: Nissim Ezekiel's Recent Poetry," *Osmania Journal of English Studies.* 13, 1 (1977): 29-43.

——. "The Achievement of R. Parthasarathy," *Chandrabhaga* 3 (Summer 1980): 49-74.

Singh, Khushwant. "After The Raj," *New Statesman.* (10 Sept. 1960): 347-49.

Singh, Kripal, Ed. *Through Different Eyes.* Calcutta: Writers Workshop, 1984.

Singh, R.K. *Indian English Writing.* New Delhi: Bahri Publications, 1987.

Singh, Satyanarayan, "Ramanujan and Ezekiel," *Osmania Journal of English Studies.* Vol. 5, No. 1 (1969): 67-75.

Sinha, Krishna Nandan, Ed. *Indian Writing in English.* New Delhi: Heritage Publishers, 1979.

Sivaramkrishna, M. "No Longer An Adjunct," Review of Nissim Ezekiel's *Hymns in Darkness*, A.K. Ramanujan's *Selected Poems*, K.N. Daruwalla's *Crossing of Rivers* and Shiv K. Kumar's *Subterfuges. Indian Book Chronicle.* (1 April 1977): 123-24, Vol. 3.

——. "That Last Refinement of Speech: The Poetry of R. Parthasarathy," *The Literary Criterion.* 12, 2-3 (1976): 151-72.

——. "The 'Tongue in English Chain', Indo-English Poetry Today," *Osmania Journal of English Studies.* 13, 1 (September 1977): 217-54.

Sreenivasan, S. "Irony in A.K. Ramanujan's Poetry," *Journal of Literature and Aesthetics.* 2, 4 (October 1982): 109-15.

Srinath, C.N. "Contemporary Indian Poetry in English," *The Literary Criterion.* 8, 2 (Summer 1968): 55-66.

——. "The Poetry of A.K. Ramanujan," *Studies in Contemporary Indo-English Verse.* Ed. A.N. Dwivedi. Bareilly: Prakash Book Depot, 1984, 29-34.

Srivastava, A.K. and Smita Sinha. "New Voices: Animadversions on Recent Indo-Anglian Poetry," *Indian Writing in English,*

Ed. K.N. Sinha. New Delhi: Heritage Publishers, 1979: 109-27.

Subrahmanian, K. "Penchant For The Florie," *Indian Writing in English*, Ed. Ramesh Mohan. Madras: Orient Longman, 1978, 203-06.

Tambimuttu. "Poetry in India: Its Heritage and New Directions," *The Atlantic Monthly*. 192, 4 (October 1953): 147-48.

Taranath, Rajeev and Meena Belliapa. *The Poetry of Nissim Ezekiel*. Calcutta: Writers Workshop, 1966.

Taranath, Rajeev. "Nissim Ezekiel," *Contemporary Indian Poetry in English*, Ed. Saleem Peeradina. Bombay: Macmillan and Co., 1972: 1-5.

Trivedi, Harish and Meenakshi Mukherjee Eds. *Interrogating Post-Colonialism: Theory, Text and Context*. Shimla: Indian Institute of Advanced Studies, 1996.

Tyrner, A.G. "Indo-Anglian Literature and The Indian Elite," *Cornell Journal of Social Relations*. 1, 1 (1966): 25-32.

——. "Uncommon Wealth," *Times Literary Supplement*. 17 September 1964: 859.

Upadhyay, M.N. "A.K. Ramanujan," *The Illustrated Weekly India*. 97, 29 (18 July 1976): 21-23.

Vaish, Y.N. "A.K. Ramanujan: An Escapist?" *Thought*. (21 June 1969): 14-15.

Verghese, C. Paul. "Indian Poetry in English Today," *The Indian P.E.N.* 40, 2-3 (February/March 1974): 1-6.

——. "The Poetry of Nissim Ezekiel," *Indian Literature*. 15, 1 (March 1972): 63-75.

——. *Problems of The Indian Creative Writer in English*. Bombay: Somaiya Publications, 1971.

Verma, K.D. "Myth and Imagery in The Unfinished Man: A Critical Reading," *Journal of South Asian Literature*. 11, 3-4 (Spring/Summer 1976): 229-38.

Verma, S.K. "A Linguist's View of English in India," *India and Foreign Review*. 15 October 1972: 20-21.

Viswanathan, Gauri. *Masks of Conquest: Literary Study and British Rule in India*. London: Faber, 1990.

Walsh, William. "In A Backward Place," Review of Nissim Ezekiel's *Hymns in Darkness. Times Literary Supplement.* (3 February 1978): 122.

——. "Small Scale Observations on Large Subject," *Aspects of Indian Writing in English.* Ed. M.K. Naik. New Delhi: Macmillan and Co., 1979: 107-19.

——. "Modern Writing in English," *India and Foreign Review.* 15 October 1972: 17-19.

——. *A Human Idiom: Literature and Humanity.* London: Chatto and Windus, 1964.

——. *A Manifold Voice: Studies in Commonwealth Literature.* London: Chatto and Windus, 1970.

——. Ed. *Readings in Commonwealth Literature.* London: Oxford University Press, 1973.

——. *The Illustrated Weekly of India.* London: Orient Longman, 1990.

——. "Two Indian Poets: Ezekiel and Parthasarathy," *The Literary Criterion.* 11, 3 (Winter 1974): 1-16.

Watson, F. "English Poetry from India," *The Listener.* (28 September 1950): 429-30.

Wendt, Allan. "Babu To Sahib: Contemporary Indian Literature," *South Atlantic Quarterly.* 64 (Winter 1965): 166-80.

William, H. Moore. "English Writing in Free India (1947-1967)," *Twentieth Century Literature.* 16, 1 (January 1970): 3-15.

William, Raymond. *Culture and Society: 1780-1950.* London: Harmondsworth, 1963.

William, H.M. *Indo-Anglian Literature 1800-1970: A Survey.* Bombay: Orient Longman, 1977.

Wiseman, Christopher, "The Development of Technique in The Poetry of Nissim Ezekiel," *Journal of South Asian Literature.* 11, 3-4 (Spring/Summer 1976): 241-52.

Young, J.C. *Postcolonialism: An Historical Introduction.* Blackwell, 2001.

Young, Veron. "Poetry Chronicle," *The Hudson Review.* 29, 4 (Winter 1976-77): 616-18.

Zinnes, Harriet. "Review of *The Striders* by A.K. Ramanujan," *Parrie Schooner.* 41, 3 (Fall 1967): 353-54.